Valsalva's Maneuver

Bubbly

Valsalva's Maneuver

Mots Justes and Indispensable Terms

John Train

Illustrated by Pierre Le-Tan

1817

An Edward Burlingame Book
HARPER & ROW, PUBLISHERS
New York, Grand Rapids, Philadelphia, St. Louis,
San Francisco, London, Singapore, Sydney, Tokyo, Toronto

First Edition
Designed by Katy Homans
Typeset by Michael & Winifred Bixler

Library of Congress Cataloging-in-Publication Data

Train, John.
  Valsalva's maneuver: mots justes and indispensable terms/John Train; illustrated by Pierre Le-Tan.
    p. cm.
  ISBN 0-06-016185-X
1. English language—Terms and phrases. 2. Vocabulary.
I. Title.
PE1689.T73   1989
428.1—dc20   89-45072

89 90 91 92 93 MPC 7 6 5 4 3 2 1

Contents

Acknowledgments

My thanks to Sara Perkins for overall collaboration, and to Timothy Dickinson, George Herrick, Susan McGrath and Piers Dixon for suggestions.

Oeil de boeuf

Introduction

Noah Webster, of the dictionary, achieved a happy use of the *mot juste*. The family had a pretty and flirtatious cook, to whom Webster could not resist giving a little affectionate pat from time to time as he passed through the kitchen.

His wife once came upon them in ardent embrace, Webster covering the cook's face with kisses. "Noah!" gasped his wife. "Noah! What are you doing! I'm surprised!" The great lexicographer looked up at his wife and addressed her sternly. "No, no, my dear, no, no, no! *You* are *astonished. I* am surprised."

It is curiously satisfying to learn the exact word for a familiar idea, often the jargon of some craft or profession, which otherwise might require considerable explanation. I took the editor of this volume, Ed Burlingame, for a sail in Maine when we were considering its form. Looking at some passing boats, he asked about the longitudinal furrow on their sides, just below the deck. "The cove stripe," I murmured. We seemed to have made progress just by invoking the term. Many religions hold that things only exist when they get named, and it is certainly much easier to handle abstractions when they can be expressed neatly.

This collection does not try to be either balanced or complete. It is just a ramble, skewed toward subjects I happen to be familiar with and expressions I have on tap. It is thus idiosyncratic, even arbitrary.

The basic terms for each category are generally not included; rather, those that someone acquainted with a subject might have encountered but not quite remember exactly, such as Bacon's idols or the basic legal writs. I have favored terms that are both interesting and amusing, but most appear just because I like them.

I trust that the reader can distinguish between the lead-in stories that are factual, which contain dates or sources, and the ones I invented, which don't.

—J.T.

Advertising

Colgate startled the Francophone world when it launched a toothpaste called Cue, which in French means a most delicate component of the female anatomy. An American airline in Brazil heavy-upped the "rendezvous lounges" in its jets until discovering that in Portuguese this means a place to make love. Chevrolet's Nova sales in Latin America were not helped by the word's meaning in Spanish: "It won't run." And Pepsi-Cola discovered that its tag line in Japanese meant "It brings your ancestors back from the dead"—which convinced no one.

bleed across the gutter: Print a picture across two pages.

button: The last line of a commercial ("We clobbered them with the button").

dinks: Dual Income, No Kids: a prime audience.

donut: A gap in a radio ad to permit local announcements ("We'll build a slug into the donut"—a local announcement in a radio spot).

drive time: When commuters are listening to their car radios.

fringe time: Brackets drive time, and includes "early fringe" and "late fringe."

heavy-up (noun or verb): A concentrated campaign: one with high weight or GRP (gross rating point) levels. Thus, "We'll launch the campaign with a heavy-up," or "We'll heavy-up the campaign."

Lubbock: This modest agglomeration is displacing East Pancake, which displaced Podunk, as the archetypal backwater: "Will it play in Lubbock, Texas?" Or, "The yahoos in East Pancake will never get it."

snipe or swipe: Diagonal (dog-ear) or other (e.g., starburst) over-printing in an advertisement.

tag line: The slogan in an ad ("Thank you, PaineWebber").

Antilogies

Antilogy is my term for a word that means two opposite things. Here are a few from a large collection.

aman (Arabic): Trifle; big deal.

apparent: Clearly so; an illusion ("apparent wind" in sailing).

boned: Containing bones (corset stays); without bones (filet of fish).

buckle: Fasten together; fall apart.

charterer: Provider; user.

chaire (Greek): Hail; farewell. The runner who brought the tidings of Marathon to Athens gasped out, *"Chairete, chairete* (rejoice), *chairete,"* and died. This sounds too pat, but it must be considered that he had ample time to compose his announcement.

cleave: Chop apart; stick together.

close: Put out of operation; put into operation (a business deal).

continue: Proceed; (legal) defer proceeding.

critical: Opposed; an essential support ("His speech was critical").

to a degree: Somewhat; greatly.

didd (Arabic; plural, **addad**): Opposite; the same.

downhill (particularly, going —): Getting worse; getting better ("It's downhill from here on").

draw (curtain): Pull closed; pull open.

dust: Remove dust; lay down dust (with nutmeg, or crop-dusting).

engagement: (Matrimonial) loving tie; (military) battle.

fariba (Arabic): Be sad; be joyful.

farouche (French): Ferocious; timid.

fast: Moving rapidly; not moving ("make fast" or "stand fast").

fight with: Fight against; fight together with.

finish (verb): Perfect (furniture); destroy.

fix: Repair; (colloq.) destroy ("I'll fix him").

handicap: Disadvantage; advantage ("I'll give you a handicap").

heave to: (Of sailor) get going; (of sailboat) halt.

hit: Success; failure ("take a hit").

horned: Possessing horns; (cattle) with horns removed.

let (double antilogy): (a) Permit; obstruct (as in tennis and "let or hindrance"). (b) Supply as lessor; use as lessee.

let him have it: Grant his desire; (slang) abuse (even murder) him.

liberal: (U.S.) in favor of government intervention; (elsewhere) against government intervention.

lose no time in . . . : Do promptly; not do at all. (When sent unsolicited tomes, Henry James is said to have liked to reply, "I shall lose no time in reading your book.")

marketing: Selling; (household) buying.

moot (double antilogy): (a) Under consideration; not under consideration. (b) Undecided; (law) decided.

overlook: Watch over; fail to watch over.

oversight: Supervision; failure to supervise.

peer: An equal; (Am. colloq.) a superior.

peinard (French): Idler; hard worker.

pharmakon (Greek): Remedy; poison.

pinch hitter: Superior substitute (baseball); inferior substitute (all other usages, notably a replacement speaker).

qualified: Just right (job applicant); defective (approval, auditor's report, etc.).

quite: Slightly ("quite nice"); utterly ("quite out of the question").

ravel: Tangle (as in sleeve of care); untangle.

renter: Landlord; tenant.

riddler: Propounder of riddles; solver of riddles.

rock: Immovable support (Rock of Ages); (music) hysterical agitation.

salut (French): Hail; farewell.

sanction: Permission; punishment.

seeded: Having seeds; with seeds removed.

several: Numerous; single ("joint and several").

smash: (Theater) triumph; (vehicle) disaster.

stand: Stay still; move ("stand out to sea," or "stand for Parliament").

sugoi (Japanese): Ghastly; superb.

table: (Parliamentary) bring up for discussion; defer discussing.

temper: Harden; soften (justice with mercy).

throw out: (Idea) propose; reject (baby with bathwater).

to top: Increase (a record, or a sundae by adding whipped cream); decrease (a tree).

trim: Cut down; embellish (turkey or Christmas tree).

unbending: Rigid; easing off from rigidity.

untouchable: Eminent beyond criticism; at the bottom of the heap.

vaquer (French): Be occupied; be unoccupied.

wind up: Prepare to start (pitchers and watches); prepare to stop (companies).

you can't be too . . . (thin): Be as thin as possible; don't get too thin.

Architecture

Stanford White (1853–1906), of McKim, Mead, and White, the celebrated New York architectural firm, specialized in huge neo-Renaissance structures. Many New York clubs—the Century, the Racquet, the University—are Florentine palazzi of his design. He had the admirable gift of creating spaces where you feel happy, and was himself a noted *bon vivant*. Alas, in a jealous dispute over the favors of a lively lady called Evelyn Nesbit, Harry K. Thaw, her husband, blasted White in the roof garden of the old Madison Square Garden building as, on stage, the performers sang "I Could Have Loved a Million Girls."

Anyway, in 1892 McKim, Mead, and White built the Boston Public Library, a noble edifice. Public buildings often display the preeminent names in the art or science to which the structure is dedicated. So McKim, Mead, and White incised into the library's facade the names of fourteen immortals:

Moses	Mozart	Wren
Cicero	Euclid	Herrick
Kalidasa	Aeschylus	Irving
Isocrates	Dante	Titian
Milton		Erasmus

There was as always some pettifogging about the particular selection. Were Robert Herrick and Washington Irving really greater authors than Homer and Shakespeare, for example? With the passage of time, however, the masterful logic of McKim, Mead, and White's choices became all too apparent. Connecting the first letters of the geniuses in each vertical column spelled out the most sublime names of all:

MCKIM   MEAD   WHITE.

charrette: For architectural students, a major examination. In the old days the model you prepared for the Beaux Arts was picked up by a small cart or **charrette** that came by each student's lodgings in turn. Thus **en charrette** for "at the last minute": sometimes the students were still applying the finishing touches as the cart joggled along.

demising wall: A boundary wall, particularly in a structure.

entablature: The three divisions of the upper section of a classical order: cornice, frieze, and architrave.

gambrel roof: In America, a roof that folds down in the middle, and then folds down again on both sides (called in England a **mansard roof**).

machicolation: Projecting section around the top of a castle, with holes in the floor for dropping stones, boiling oil, or whatever on attackers.

mullion: Strip dividing window panes.

oeil de boeuf: "Bull's-eye": small circular window.

pilaster: A flat column, projecting only slightly from a wall.

porte cochère: Door with a porch wide enough to admit wheeled vehicles.

rustication: Stonework with deeply incised joins.

soffit: What you see when you look up at a beam, arch, staircase, or other structural element from below.

volute: The spiral ornament on an Ionic capital. So called for resemblance to the spiral in shells of the family Volutidae.

Art

Berenson, like a pig sniffing truffles beneath an oak, sensed something under the *ottocento* madonna—*pentimento*, perhaps? A few hours' work by Signor Naldo confirmed the possibility. *"Dunque, andiamo, Naldo* [Let's give it a try]," said Berenson.

Some months later, returning from Boston, Berenson once more visited the little shop in Via dei Bardi to see how things were progressing. *"Mica male,"* said Naldo noncommittally, pronouncing it "miha." Behind the figures another form was gradually appearing . . . yes!

Peering at the canvas with his flashlight and *loupe,* Berenson realized that bit by bit was faintly emerging not a Giorgione, not even a Titian, but the dim outlines of a heroic equestrian portrait of Mussolini! *"Lo preferisco com'era,"* he said, casually, *"Rimetiamolo a posto."* ["I prefer it the way it was. Let's go back to where we were."]

Naldo, expressionless, nodded.

aerial (or atmospheric or color) perspective: A way of showing distance: remote objects look paler, bluer, and fuzzier than close ones.

contrapposto: Chest and shoulders face in one direction, with hips and legs twisted to face in another.

églomisé: Reverse painting on glass (from Glomy, eighteenth-century French decorator).

genre art: Popular scenes.

Hogarth frame: Has two lines of gold beading with a scooped black channel between.

objet de vertù: Small, precious object.

parure: Set of jewelry.

pentimento: Traces of an earlier work underneath a painting.

pinchbeck: Imitation gold, an alloy of copper and zinc; more generally, a cheap counterfeit.

quattrocento, cinquecento, etc.: The fourteen hundreds, fifteen hundreds, etc.

sang de boeuf: "Bull's blood," i.e., oxblood: a deep, brilliant red glaze used in Chinese pottery.

Auctions

hammer price: The price at which an object is sold in the sales-room.

knockoff: The ritual—often in a café near the auction house—in which a ring distributes to its members the objects they have acquired at a sale.

ring: A group of dealers who prevent buyers in a salesroom from getting any desirable object at a reasonable price. The members do not bid against each other.

table price: The price at which an object is redistributed to a ring member in the knockoff.

Entrechat

Ballet

arabesque: The dancer stands on one leg with the other extended backward, knee straight.

ballerina: For ballet people, the ballerina is the principal female performer in a piece, usually the only one allowed to wear jewelry. The others are dancers.

ballon: A soft, bouncy, flying quality in leaping, often found among somewhat bowlegged dancers.

entrechat: A leap during which the dancer crosses his feet a number of times, often beating them together.

fouetté: The dancer stands on her left leg. The raised right leg whips her around and around like a top.

Boontling

Boontling is a language . . . created by the early residents of upper Anderson Valley in Mendocino County, California. In his book Boontling: An American Lingo, *Charles C. Adams termed it " . . . a deliberately contrived jargon which was spoken extensively between 1880 and 1920." Writing about it in the* Christian Science Monitor, *Raymond A. Lajoie said, "When spoken, it sounds like English that is not quite understandable, like a kind of double-double talk. . . . When written, it looks like someone used a typewriter with his fingers crossed."*

One of the reasons the language was created was to allow adults to gossip without fear of their children or outsiders understanding. As a result, Adams reports, approximately 15 percent of the language was made up of "nonch harpins"—objectionable talk.

Paul Dickson, *Words*

afe: A fart.

burlap: To have sexual intercourse, sometimes *burl.* Other words for the same act: *bow* and *geech.*

dreef: Interrupted coitus.

keeboarp: Premature ejaculation.

moldunes: Breasts.

squirrel ribby: An erect penis.

British Family Names

There are some standard differences between American and English pronunciation. First, final *-ham* is in England an unaccented *-um*. Second, Americans usually assume that an unfamiliar *o* should be pronounced as in box, even though they are aware of mother, money, and Monday. So such names as Constable (pronounced Cùnstable) are confusing.

Then, the English *er* is usually pronounced *ah*. A man who could write was once called (and written) Clark; the spelling changed but not, in England, the pronunciation, whence Berkeley, Derby, etc. Next comes *y* and *ʒ*. The *y* in ye (as in ye olde) represents an extinct letter pronounced *th*, while the *ʒ* in Menzies and Dalzell stands for a Scottish letter close in pronunciation to *y*. Then, sometimes final *s* is rendered *ys*, *yss*, or *is*, as in Pepys or Glamis; the final vowel in such instances is silent.

Also, Americans move the accent in unfamiliar surnames to the rear even when they don't belong there, as with Sophia Loren and Muhammad Ali, while the accent in English surnames often drifts forward, as in Vanbrugh (Vànbra) or Lascelles (Làssells).

Abergavenny:
  Abergènny (hard g)
Alnwick: Annick
Auchinleck:
  Afflèck, Ockinleck
Beauchamp: Beecham
Beaufort: Bòfoot
Beaulieu: Biew-li

Belvoir: Beava
Bethune: Beaton
Bolingbroke: Bullingbrook
Buccleuch: Bucklòo
Caius: Keys (College)
Calverley: Cahvaly
Capell: Cayple
Carnegie: Cahnèggie

Cecil: Sissil (Salisbury)
Cholmondely: Chumley
Cirencester: Sista
Cockburn: Coèbun
Colquhoun: Cahòon
Courthope: Coht-hope
Cowper: Cooper
Dalyell or Dalzell:
  Dee-èl (usually)
De Crespigny: De Crèppni
De la Warr: Like the state
Elgin: Elgin (hard g)
Fermor: Fahma
ffolkes: Foaks
Gifford: Jiffud
Glamis: Glahms
Gower: Gaw
Harewood: Hahwood
Heathcoat: Hethcut
Hepburn: Heb'n
Hertford: Hahfud
Hobart: Hùbud
Home: Hume
Inveraray: Inveraira
Islay: Eye-la
Kirkcudbright: Kukòobri
Knollys: Nowles
Lascelles: Làssells
Leominster: Lemsta
Leveson-Gower:
  Loosun-Gaw
Magdalen: Màwdlin
Magrath: Magràh

Mainwaring: Mannering
Marjoribanks:
  Marshbanks
Marlborough:
  Màwlbra
McGillicuddy:
  Màclicuddy
Menzies:
  Mìngiz (Scotland)
Montgomery: Mungùmri
Newburgh: Newbra
Northcote: Nàwthcut
Pytchley: Pìe-chley
Rhys: Rees (usually)
Rotherhithe: Redriff
Roxburghe: Roxbra
Ruthven: Rivven
St. Clair: Sinclair
St. John: Sìnjun
St. Leger: Sìllinja
Shrewsbury: Shrowsbry
Southwark: Sùthuk
Stanhope: Stannup
Strabolgi:
  Strabòwgie (hard g)
Towcaster: Taoster
Trevelyan: Trevìllian
Urquhart: Uhkut
Vanbrugh: Vànbra
Wemyss: Weems
Westmorland: Wèsmlund
Woburn: Woobun
Wodehouse: Woodhouse

Carving

We still talk about *dismembering* a cadaver; you once did the same for a hen or a heron (but not a bittern or a crane). Here are some of the old terms:

GAME

You: **untache** a beaver
unjoint a bittern
sesche or **leach** a boar
sauce or **break** a capon
fruche or **fract** a chicken
unlace a coney (rabbit)
display a crane
untache or **unlatch** a curlew
break a deer, egret, or hare
rear a goose
spyle a ham
dismember or **spoil** a hen

dismember a heron
shoulder a lamb or kid
unbrace a mallard
display or **wing** a partridge
disfigure a peacock
allay a pheasant
side a pig
thigh a pigeon
  or other small bird
mince or **quinse** a plover
display or **wing** a quail
lift a swan
thigh a woodcock

FISH

You: **tuske** a barbel
splay a bream
frush or **fin** a chub
tame a crab
transon, trounson,
  truncheon or **trassene**
  an eel
side a haddock
string a lamprey

barbe a lobster
splat a pike
sauce a plaice
undertranch a porpoise
lyste or **chine** a salmon
tranch a sturgeon
sauce a tench
culpon or **gobbet** a trout
undertranch a tuna

The City (i.e., London Financial District)

A London colleague describes calling his broker in New York to ask about a hot new stock issue. "I know all about it. It's going to bomb," said the New York broker. My friend put in a large order. The issue collapsed. My friend lost a lot of money. Furiously, he called the broker, who said, "But I told you it was going to bomb!" It took some time for them to realize that "bomb" means go *up* in England and *down* in New York.

apostrophe: British business usage often drops it: e.g., "Hambros." Lloyds (bank) can thus be distinguished from Lloyd's (insurance).

the Bank: The bank of England.

barrister: Trial lawyer who will also render opinions on specialized points of law. Technically, he is engaged ("briefed") by the solicitor, q.v., through whom he and the client communicate.

counsel: Always refers to a barrister, not a solicitor.

crossed check: Check with two lines across the face, which cannot be cashed by a third party, only deposited by payee. This device, which is also customary in France, should be adopted in the United States.

be gazumped: Lose a house or deal to a higher offer after an oral agreement.

guinea: Unit of payment (21 shillings) used for a few elegant transactions, such as in buying a horse; formerly also in wagers, portrait painter's bills, and some doctors' fees.

name (at Lloyd's): A nonworking member who by joining **syndicates** risks all his assets.

Q.C. (queen's counsel): A distinguished barrister (not solicitor) who after applying for and receiving this title ("taking silk") only appears in court "supported" by an assistant (or "junior," who may be seventy years old) and charges much higher fees. Often called a "silk" or "senior counsel."

solicitor: Attorney whom you engage ("instruct") for general purposes in England, who may not plead in the High Court. Often without law school training; has always served as an articled clerk.

syndicate (Lloyd's): The manager of a Lloyd's syndicate accepts participations from **names** in the syndicate's risks and profits. He then commits the syndicate to tiny fractions of a large variety of risks presented to him by brokers.

v. ("vee"): Versus, as in Kramer v. Kramer.

Crime

Just behind us on Exeter Street lived a well-known Boston spinster, Miss Ella Day by name. One moonlight night, when I was about ten years old, I was aroused by the noise of a watchman's rattle and hurried to the window hoping to catch sight of the burglar leaping over the back-yard fences. Although I could see no burglar, I did see Miss Day's attenuated right arm projecting from her window with the rattle, which she was vigorously whirling, at the end of it. Thoroughly thrilled, I called across to her:

"Miss Day! Miss Day! What is it? Robbers?"

Even now I can hear her thin shaking voice with its slightly condescending acerbity:

"No—burglars!"

In those days Boston was Boston.

Arthur Train, *Puritan's Progress*

borgata: The territory of a Mafia family.

bulletproof: Under such heavy police surveillance that he is hard to murder.

cooping: Sleeping on duty, usually in a patrol car. The practice follows from permitting patrolmen to take off-duty jobs. It is justified by the police as creating a pattern that malefactors can't predict: "The best collars are made coming off the coop."

cross juice: When a bookmaker succeeds in having some of his customers bet at, for instance, 4-to-5 on Seabiscuit to win, and other customers an equal amount at 4-to-5 on Seabiscuit to lose, so that he makes money either way.

drop a dime (on): Inform on.

felony flyers: Sneakers.

get in the car: Join in becoming an informer, in exchange for reduction or remission of sentence.

juice man: Person in the criminal justice system with whom criminals make deals—to become informers, etc.

made man or guy, wise guy, button: Mafia member.

the Mafia hierarchy: From the top down: **boss, underboss, consigliere, capo, soldier, associate.** An initiate or "made" member, who has usually committed a murder, is described as **"a friend of ours"** when being introduced by one Mafioso to another; an associate is **"a friend of mine."**

make your bones: Carry out a murder to qualify for Mafia membership.

O.R.: Own recognizance: released without bail pending trial.

stall: Distracts the victim while the **hook** takes the wallet, handbag, briefcase or whatever.

tuna: Partly non-Italian Mafioso.

vigorish ("the vig"); also **juice:** Usurious interest.

Croquet

A Match at Winterthur

My partner was Herbert Bayard Swope, and the opponents Eleonora Duse and Walter Lippmann. She was using the new "between the legs" stroke, somewhat frowned on in good croquet circles, particularly among ladies of quality.

Swope succeeded in knocking La Duse's ball through the three final hoops and into the terminal stake. "A triple peel," he proclaimed with satisfaction.

He then announced loudly that since he had "pegged her out," for the rest of the game she could only play one stroke in three. "*O dio, son perduta,*" wailed the diva. Swope refrained from hitting the stake himself and returned to mess up poor Walter Lippmann.

Perhaps hoping to weaken Swope's concentration, Walter turned red and clutched his chest, simulating a cardiac disorder. Swope was remorseless, smashing Walter's ball twenty yards to the boundary. He then addressed himself to La Duse, who, uttering a piercing cry, collapsed full length on the green, as she had a thousand times on the stage.

"Default!" cried Swope.

baulk: Where play starts.

jump stroke: A downward hit to make your ball jump over the other ball.

peeling: Putting a partner's or opponent's ball through the final hoops (three, for a triple) to peg it out. Named for Walter H. Peel, who formed the United All England Croquet Association in 1896–1897.

peg out: Hit the terminal stake. Once pegged out, you can take only one turn in three.

rolling croquet: Hitting the ball near the top, with sustained pressure, to give it "follow."

roquet: Hit another ball with yours.

rover: A player who has run all the hoops but not struck the winning peg.

rover hoop: The last hoop.

stop stroke: A short, sharp tap when taking croquet: the player's ball goes only a short distance, the other much farther.

take croquet: After hitting another ball, you get two shots. With the first you can take croquet: hit your ball and the other simultaneously. Some rules allow holding down your ball with your foot so that the shot only moves the other ball.

turning peg: The stake at the halfway point of the course.

wicketed: Halfway through the hoop.

wiring: Leaving an opponent's ball with either a hoop or peg between it and all other balls.

English English

"We'll be staying at the Claridge's Hotel."

"No, no, no," said Lord Biedermeier. "Simply say Claridge's. Not the Claridge's. Nor Claridge's Hotel either. Oh, dear me, no. Just say Claridge's."

"What difference does it make?" asked Elias.

"These are the little signals by which people like us recognize each other," said Lord Biedermeier.

Dominick Dunne, *People Like Us*

Are you through?: Visitors to Britain are puzzled when the operator ("telephonist") through whom they are placing a long distance ("trunk") call asks if they are "through." "No!" howls the visitor. At this, the operator is likely to disconnect him and start over. She is asking if the call has *gotten* through, not if he is through talking.

balls-up: Mess (from hard lumps of snow forming under horses' hooves).

Barbour: The universal English country foul-weather jacket, made of oiled cotton by this firm.

Boxing Day: First day after Christmas. (A Christmas box is now any gift, in cash or kind, to service personnel; at one time these were placed in a box.)

bugger all: Nothing.

> *Judge:* Prisoner, have you anything to say before I pass sentence upon you?
>
> *Prisoner (softly):* Bugger all.
>
> *Judge to bailiff:* What did he say?
>
> *Bailiff:* He said bugger all, M'Lud.
>
> *Judge:* Odd. I was almost sure he said something.

the Cinque Ports: Originally, Dover, Hastings, Hythe, Romney, and Sandwich; later Winchelsea and Rye as well. Enjoyed special rights in return for furnishing ships and men for coastal defense. Wellington, Curzon, and Churchill, among others, were wardens of the Cinque Ports.

county family: Eminent regional family.

Harley Street: Traditional abode of the grander English doctors, particularly surgeons and other specialists (called "Mr."). (G.P.'s are "Dr.")

lavatory: "Proper" word for toilet. See **loo** and **W. C.**

leader-writer: Editorialist.

loo: Toilet. See **lavatory** and **W.C.** "Loo" probably comes from *lieu*, "place," or *l'eau*, "water"—both French (as, indeed, is "toilet" —the *toilette*, "little cloth" on which a lady arranged her effects on a bedside table).

money for jam: Easy pickings.

Norfolk-Howard: Slang for bug. (On June 26, 1826, a man called Bugg changed his name to Norfolk-Howard.)

Oxbridge: Of Oxford and/or Cambridge, e.g., accent. Other universities are "red brick" or "plate glass" (built since about 1960).

public school: A private school.

recusant (family): Old Catholics.

rushing his fences: Coming on too strong.

Savile Row: The London street where traditionally the best tailors are found: Huntsman, Henry Poole, and so on. My own, who works from dowdy premises in Pimlico, for years kept "of Savile Row" on his labels.

talking suit: Well-dressed nitwit.

ticktock: A tiresome enthusiast.

too clever by half: Too smart for his own good.

W. C.: For water closet. Old-fashioned term for toilet. See **lavatory** and **loo**.

Wellingtons ("wellies," also called "gum boots"): In England it rains constantly. To take a walk in the country you need rubber boots to negotiate the ever-present mud. The preferred type are green. They cover the calf and no longer resemble the boots worn by the duke of Wellington, which can be seen in miniature in the Lobb store in St. James's Street. The English are amazed to learn that one rarely needs wellies in America.

Falconry

How oft, with loving hand,
Have I the Pelt *for* Falcon-gentle *held!—*
Then fed, she rouzed *and* mantled; *and anon*
Feaked *on my glove, while I did smooth her* mailes,
Her petty-single *with a soft plume touched;*
Meanwhile, with right good will, she pruned *herself.—*
Full oft I told her of a Hern at seidge:
Then were we friends; and when the drousy night
Talked to the world of stars in its bright dreams,
I loved to deem she jouketh *well in it.*

"N. C.," quoted in C. E. Hare, *The Language of Field Sports*

the traditional hawking hierarchy:
An **eagle** for an emperor
A **gyrfalcon** for a king
A **peregrine** for an earl
A **bustard** or **buzzard** for a lord
A **merlin** for a lady
A **saker** or **sackeret** for a knight
A **lanner** or **lanneret** for a squire
A **hobby** for a young squire
A **goshawk** for a yeoman
A **sparrowhawk** for a priest
A **muskyte** for "an holiwater clerke"
A **kestrel** for a servant

barefaced: Unhooded.

bind: Pull down prey from the air.

falcon: From Latin *falx*, sickle, referring to the curve of the beak. Means a female; a male is called a **tiercel.**

-gentle: Suffix indicating a trained bird.

jess: Leg strap to tie a leash on.

jouk or jenk: Sleep.

lure: Bait made of feathers and meat, used to recall a hawk.

mailes: Breast feathers.

mews: Where falcons are kept. The Royal Stables, and later the National Gallery, were built on the site of the former Royal Mews.

mutes: Droppings.

pelt: A falcon's victim.

pounces: Claws.

sails: Wings.

stoop: Dive on prey.

Flying

air side (land side): In an airport, you are always either on the land side (toward the terminal) or the air side (toward the plane) of the system of gates and other barriers.

getting behind the curve: When a plane climbs too steeply, inviting a stall.

hidden city (or fictional point) ticketing: Writing a ticket to a place beyond the real destination to produce a lower fare. The route includes a stop at the intended city. The round-trip fare is lowered, often because of currency advantages, since you pay in zlotys, or whatever.

Food

"Who *was* this Al Dante?" asked the man in the tight suit. The headwaiter smiled vaguely, remembered urgent concerns elsewhere, and vanished.

à l'ail: With garlic.

à la Dieppoise: With mussels and shrimp.

al dente: (Of spaghetti) "toothy," quite hard—the way it should be, for an Italian.

amuse-gueule: "Amuse-face": an appetizer.

à point, saignant, bleu: (Of meat) well done, rare, very rare: literally, "to the point," "bleeding," "blue."

baveuse: Runny, notably soufflés, omelettes, and Camembert.

bechamel: White cream sauce.

Bercy: With shallots and parsley.

bigarade: Flavored with orange.

billibi: Mussel soup with white wine and cream. (Named after Billy Baldwin.)

bolognese: With meat sauce.

boula boula: Turtle soup with peas and cream.

bourgignon: With red wine, onions, bacon, and mushrooms.

chantilly: Vanilla-flavored cream with sugar.

chasseur: With tomatoes, mushrooms, parsley, and shallots.

en croûte: Baked in a crust.

farci: Stuffed.

florentine: With spinach.

forestière: With wild mushrooms, bacon and potatoes.

au gratin: With a cheese or bread crumb crust.

julienne: In narrow strips.

macédoine (de fruits): A mixture (fruit cocktail).

marengo: With tomatoes (from the gory battlefield of Marengo) etc.

Milanese: With cheese.

mit Schlag (or just **mit**): With whipped cream.

mongole (*potage*): Pea and tomato.

Montmorency: With cherries.

niçoise: With olives, anchovies, capers, etc.

provençale: With tomato sauce containing garlic.

savory: The end of an old-fashioned English meal: anchovies or scrambled eggs on little disks of toast; or perhaps "devils on horseback"—prunes wrapped in bacon.

vapeur: Steamed.

French

Marcel Proust (1871–1922) heard that the duc de Gramont (who appears in *Remembrance of Things Past* as the ponderous duc de Guermantes) was holding a splendid weekend shooting party for royalty and other grandees at his country house, Vallière, outside Paris.

Proust was eager to describe such a fête in his book, and so launched frenzied appeals to get himself invited, swearing that he would stay out of the way, would only observe in silence, and so on. Most reluctantly, the duke consented.

At the end of the final lunch the *livre d'or* was passed around the table. The royalty signed with their Christian names and brief comments.

Proust eyed the book avidly as it wormed its way toward him, enchanted to record his name among this exalted host, and primed to eclipse their banalities with a brilliant comment. The duke, however, was dismayed at such impertinence. "*Pas de pensées, Monsieur Proust*," he hissed: "No big ideas, please, just your name." Proust, white with fury, scribbled "M. Proust," withdrew as soon as possible, and rushed back to Paris.

The present duke told me the sequel. The next day arrived a long, indignant letter from Proust, setting matters straight: The duke was enormously rich and fashionable, but Proust was the glory of the age; indeed, the duke might well only be remembered in his pages, and so on.

All quite true! And when the house was sold recently it emerged, in the inventory of the contents, that this unique letter was the most valuable object in the place.

A pretentious *boulevardier* was asked if he would consent to appear in Proust's great work, in a minor but recognizable role. Unfortunately, the man was also up for election to the Jockey Club, and wished on no account to rock the boat in that quarter. *"Ca me couterait mon Jockey,"* he wailed. In an ecstasy of indecision he canvassed his friends: should he choose the club, or immortality?

In the end, after much suffering, he declined Proust's offer. Alas, the Jockey Club turned him down.

à gogo: All you want.

amitié amoureuse: The language of love, as of cuisine, is French. This delicious term describes a protracted amorous friendship.

amour de la boue: "Love of mud": used of nineteenth-century realist literature.

animateur: A technical writer who explains complex ideas in an easily understood fashion.

aubade: "Dawn song": the troubadour's sad early morning song on leaving his mistress.

au pied de la lettre: Literally; exactly.

belle laide: A woman with attractive, although irregular, features.

bien dans sa peau: "Comfortable in his skin": at ease with himself.

b.s.p. (h.s.p.): Bonne (haute) société protestante. "Good (high) protestant society": counterparts of English **recusant.**

cachet: Elegant distinction.

canard: Widely held fallacy, often one put about deliberately.

ce pays-çi: How a courtier referred to Versailles.

cinq-à-sept: "Five to seven": the traditional period of French fashionable assignations.

claire idée fausse: Convincing wrong idea.

clochard: A Paris tramp, so called because at one time the Halles, or produce market, halted business at the sound of a bell, or cloche, at which time tramps could scavenge for scraps.

comme il faut: Correct, proper.

cordon sanitaire: A barrier separating hostile or quarantined areas. Figuratively, a conversational taboo. "Don't talk about rope in the house of a hanged man," say the French.

coup de foudre: (Literally, "thunderbolt"): love at first sight.

coup de vieux: When someone, often a man, suddenly looks older.

déformation professionnelle: "My nature is subdued to what it works in, like the dyer's hand," says Shakespeare (Sonnet 111). To a policeman crime is rampant, to a doctor disease is rife, and a soldier constantly worries about attack.

dégagé: Relaxed, casual.

de rigeur: Required by fashion or custom.

dernier cri: (Literally, "latest cry"): the latest thing, implying trendiness.

"Enarque": A graduate of the French ÉNA—École Nationale d'Administration—who is usually assured a good career in the government.

épater les bourgeois: To shock the conventionally minded.

esprit de l'escalier: When a frequenter of a salon, where wit and learning were greatly prized, finally thinks of the perfect rejoinder to a rival's *mot* on the way down the staircase (*escalier*).

état d'âme: "State of soul," as distinct from mind. How someone feels deep down.

fin: Subtle, elegant, polished.

fin de race: "End of breed": a decadent, overly refined aristocrat.

le gauche caviar: Radical chic.

gens de connaissance: Persons whom one could be expected to know.

au grand galop: "At full gallop": at full tilt.

gratin: The social upper "crust."

honnête homme: Originally, in the seventeenth century, a complete gentleman, either bourgeois or aristocrat, refined but without pretentions or prejudices. Today (in quotes) accomplished gentleman; (without quotes) honest man.

ideé de base: The fundamental conception.

insortable: Someone you ought not bring to a social gathering.

jeu d'esprit: A witty sally.

jeunesse dorée: "Gilded youth."

le métier de femme: Womanly skill—in looking elegant, managing a house, bringing up children, keeping her husband happy.

mot juste: Exactly the right term for something, e.g., **Valsalva's Maneuver.**

Fin de race.

nécessaire de voyage: A seventeenth-, eighteenth-, or nineteenth-century traveling kit, often of cylindrical wood, to fit into a saddlebag.

parvenu: Also **arriviste:** newly rich. Churchill describes asking his bodyguard ("detective") as they strolled in the grounds of a country house, what he thought of *that* . . . a heated swimming pool. The detective pursed his lips judiciously. "Frankly, sir, it smacks of the parvenoo."

P.D.G.: *Président-directeur-générale:* C.E.O.

placement: The assignment of the guests' seats at a dining table.

plaque de propreté: A plate on a door to protect it from fingerprints.

poule de luxe: A high-class prostitute.

renvoyer l'ascenseur: "Send back the elevator": a reciprocal favor, i.e., a lawyer sends a client to a bank; the bank passes the lawyer some legal business.

retroussé: Of a nose: turned up at the end.

rincer les yeux: "Eyewash": said of gazing at a pretty woman or beautiful object.

rites de passage: Baptisms, weddings, funerals, sunset guns, and the like.

roman à clef: "Novel with a key": presenting actual persons in fictional guise.

sans gêne: Someone who doesn't realize that he (or often, she) is bothering others.

vieux jeu: Out of date.

Furniture

The moonlight fubbed the girandoles.

Wallace Stevens

apron piece: The ornamental, shaped portion below the seat-rail of a chair, or the underframing of tables and stands.

athénienne: Tripod holding a basin.

bergère: An easy chair with a curved padded back.

bombé: With an outward swelling: e.g., chair with flaring seat or chest of drawers with bulging front.

boule (or **boulle** or **buhl**): Inlay of metal, mother-of-pearl, tortoiseshell, etc. After André Charles Boule, seventeenth-century French cabinetmaker.

canterbury: A woman's writing desk; in England, a low stand with partitions to hold magazines and albums.

chauffeuse: A low armless chair that draws up to the fire for such purposes as pulling on stockings. Also called a slipper chair.

cheval glass: A tall, tiltable mirror between upright supports.

davenport: U.S.: large sofa; U.K.: woman's writing desk.

distressed: Beaten about, sometimes with chains, to simulate age and use.

dosser: "Backing": term applied in the Middle Ages to hangings round the walls of a hall behind the seats, and also the ornamental covering at the back of a chair.

egg-and-tongue: Egg-shaped, alternating with a dartlike ornament, also known by the Latin term "echinus" from its fancied resemblance to a sea urchin.

epergne: An elaborate dish for the center of a dining table, with compartments for fruit and nuts or for flowers.

escutcheon: Shield-shaped surface showing a coat of arms, monogram, or other device; a keyhole plate.

fretwork, cutwork, latticework: Wood cut into intricate patterns.

gadrooning, knurling, nulling: Ornamental edge.

garniture (de cheminée): Set of five vases, or perhaps vases and candlesticks, for a mantelpiece.

girandole: A branched candle holder. If mounted on a wall, may have a mirror.

linen-fold pattern: Carved ornament resembling folded cloth, used mostly for decoration of panels in woodwork and furniture; presumably originated on chests storing cloth.

marquetry: Decorative inlay of wood, ivory, mother-of-pearl, etc.

parquetry: Wood mosaic flooring.

pier glass: Long wall-mounted mirror.

raked (back): Slanted.

saber legs: Curved.

table meublée: A table, usually round, with a floor-length cloth cover.

vermiculate: With worm holes.

German

Two professors of philosophy, bowed by *Weltschmerz*, are waddling across the quad at Göttingen. One grasps the other by the elbow and asks earnestly, "Have you effer considered, *lieber kollege*, how happy are zose who have neffer been born?" The other professor nods with satisfaction as they continue their waddle; then he seizes the first professor's arm and replies, "But have *you* effer considered, *lieber kollege*, how few effer achieve ziss happy condition?"

Bettschwere: "Bed heaviness": without the energy to get up.

Bildungsroman: A novel based on the protagonist's spiritual development.

Drachenfutter: "Dragon fodder": guilty husband's present to wife.

Erminenfloh: "Ermine flea": a toady of the eminent.

Fachmensch: A narrow specialist, who makes little sense outside his area.

Feierabend: The pleasant close of a working day, with the evening to look forward to.

Fingerspitzengefühl: "Fingertipfeel": an intuitive sensibility.

fisselig: Nagged to the point of incompetence.

Gemütlichkeit: Coziness.

Gestalt: A whole greater than the sum of its parts.

Katzenjammer: A monumental hangover. Literally, "the hub-bub of mating cats."

kleiner Mensch: "Small man": narrow-minded, second-rate.

kursi: Sentimental kitsch.

pomadig: Able to slip easily through events, as though oiled.

Schadenfreude: Taking pleasure in others' troubles.

Schlimmbesserung: An improvement that makes things worse.

Stammplatz: Your favorite, usual spot, e.g., café table.

stumpf: Dull.

Torschlusspanik: "Gate closing panic": dread of missing something.

Weltschmerz: Sadness over the ills of the world, especially as an expression of romantic pessimism. "The sense of tears in mortal things."

Wundersucht: Appetite for miracles.

Zivilcourage: Courage to express unpopular opinions.

Zugzwang: In chess, when neither player can move without getting into trouble.

Zwischenraum: The space between things.

Heraldry

COLORS

argent: Silver or white

azure: Blue

gules: Red

or: Gold or yellow

purpure: Purple

sable: Black

vert: Green

LINES

bend: Diagonal from the viewer's upper left to lower right

bend sinister: Diagonal from the upper right to lower left; identifies a bastard

chevron: An inverted V

fess: Horizontal across the middle

pale: Vertical

POSITIONS OF ANIMALS AND BIRDS

couchant: Lying down

couped: Cut off—usually just the head shows

displayed: With wings and talons spread

dormant: Sleeping

guardant: Full-face

lodged: Reposing

nascent: Rising from the middle of a device

passant: Walking

rampant: Rearing

regardant: Looking back

sejant: Sitting
statant: Standing
trippant: Running
volant: Flying

These can occur in combination, e.g., passant regardant: walking, looking backward.

differencing: Varying a shield to distinguish between the branches of a family.

Hunting

Horses sound, dogs healthy
Earths stopped, and foxes plenty!

Old Toast

In 1949 my brother Jim was on the staff of a certain General Van Buskirk, stationed in Fort Lee, Virginia. The general liked the idea of hunting. He got himself properly kitted out, and studied up on the correct forms and terminologies. Alas, he was no rider and cut a poor figure in the field, in spite of his grasp of the minutiae.

Once, while hunting with the local pack along with a couple of his aides, he lost control of his horse, which ran up among the hounds, leaving the field far behind.

"General! Hold hard! Hold hard! You're riding down the goddamn hounds!" screamed one of his aides from behind.

The general, bouncing almost out of his saddle, elbows over his shoulders, turned around and with purple face howled at the aide, "Don't say that! Say, 'Ware* hounds!'"

brush: The fox's tail, once actually used as a brush.

cap: Traditionally worn by the master, hunt servants, and children; others wear top hats or bowlers.

cast: Try to recover the fox's scent.

challenge: The bark of a hound when he first scents a fox; another hound's echoing of the first bark.

Pronounced "warr."

chop: Kill a sleeping fox, or trap it in its lair.

draw: The country the master plans to hunt, whose earths have been plugged up or "stopped." A huntsman draws a covert when he has hounds look for a fox there.

earth: A fox's underground lair.

feathering: Tails wagging.

the field: The horsemen.

give tongue, speak: Cry, in pursuit of the quarry.

gone away: Hounds jump the fox and get on the line. When they are running, the huntsman sounds "gone away," and the field sets off.

hacking jacket: Tweed riding jacket with pronounced waist suppression, longer skirts than usual, and steeply slanted pockets. Preferably not worn hunting.

hold hard: A rebuke to riders who follow too closely upon hounds.

hunting: How hunters refer to their sport. Saying "fox hunting" reveals the outsider.

hunt servants: From officials to dog feeders, some paid, some not. Unpaid servants wear the bows on the back of the cap right side up, paid servants upside down.

mask: The fox's head.

mob: Surround or kill the fox before it can run.

music: The hounds' cry.

nose leather: The tip of a dog's nose.

in pink: Wearing the scarlet jacket of a senior member of the field, perhaps after the name of a London sporting tailor.

ratcatcher: Mufti—typically, black coat, tan breeches, and bowler —worn by guests and grooms who are neither members nor hunt servants.

stern: The tail end of a foxhound.

thruster: A stinker, who pushes his way through gates ahead of others, including women.

up: Mounted.

Intelligence

"Good morning, gentlemen," the lecturer began. "Today your street-work course will take up surveillance and countersurveillance. The basic technique is the ABC formation. Three agents—men and women—follow a target, usually two in line behind him and the third well back and across the street. The trackers vary their distance behind the target according to the speed he's walking and how careful he is, and rotate their positions periodically. If one is noticed by the target, or 'burned,' he's replaced by a fresh one. The whole team turns over anyway every few hours. So you use at the very least three teams of three agents—assuming eight-hour shifts—or nine individuals, to monitor a single target, plus central radio coordination and motorized agents if the target gets into a vehicle. It's a costly business.

"Then there's countersurveillance. In preparation for a sensitive meeting you may be told to pass through a long pedestrian tunnel or over a bridge or in some other way make anybody following you stand out. Your countersurveillance team, either looking backward from a fixed point or walking in the opposite direction, will try to spot the trackers. Another technique is for the agent to walk past two or three positions from which the countersurveillance team can take Polaroid snaps of the whole street, looking for any individuals who show up in all the pictures. And of course other members of the countersurveillance team cover the meeting area. Sometimes there are even cars placed in the streets leading to the meeting place to block access by the local police or by the opposing intelligence service. Any questions so far?"

Aunt Minnie

active measures, activnyye meropriyatiya (KGB): Manipulation of opinion abroad, through disinformation, controlled political and labor organizations, and agents of influence in government, the press, the churches, academia, etc., collectively called *kombinatsia*.

agent bolvan (KGB): An agent blown or sacrificed, often to establish the credibility or take the heat off another.

agentura (KGB): Spy ring.

apparat (KGB): An agent network deployed against a particular target.

Aquarium: Moscow GRU headquarters.

Aunt Minnie: Casual photograph with intelligence interest.

babbler: Puts out polyglot double-talk to baffle bugs.

bennies: World War II Italian agents, who soothed their handlers by repeating, "*Va bene, va bene* [OK, OK]."

bigot list: List of officers witting, i.e., in the know, as to a sensitive operation.

brute force: Attacking a code or cipher by applying fragments of plaintext to the encoded text, using millions of combinations per second to see if anything fits.

cacklebladder: British Secret Service lingo for a fake corpse, often covered with chicken blood, used to blackmail someone present by making him think he is an accessory to murder.

casserole (French): Informer.

chicken feed: Secrets fed to a recruit within an opposing service, or revealed by a defector, to establish bona fides.

the Cousins: British intelligence lingo for the CIA.

dangle (operation): To serve up a controlled source as bait to an opposition intelligence service for counterespionage purposes.

dead drop: Where you hide a secret message, such as a hole in masonry, at the base of a tree, or (a KGB favorite) under the seat of a public telephone.

disinformation, dezinformatsia (KGB): Forgery, black propaganda, etc.

dubok (KGB): A dead drop.

flaps and seals: CIA course in opening envelopes.

fluttering (CIA): Administering a polygraph test.

friends: British official-circles lingo for the SIS.

go-away: Signal to abort a planned contact.

grannies: Subsidized private residents of observation posts—e.g., overlooking Soviet premises—used by surveillants.

grinder (CIA): Defector debriefing facility.

GRU: Soviet military intelligence—operates parallel with KGB.

honey trap (KGB): Sexual entrapment.

JETRO: Japanese External Trade Organization, their industrial intelligence service, with offices in the U.S. and dozens of other countries.

lamplighters: British term for operation support personnel: transportation, surveillance, safe houses, etc.

maskirovka (KGB): "Deception." Receives much higher emphasis among the Soviets than in the West.

MI5, MI6: Old British designations, still used, for SS and SIS.

Minimax Fire Extinguisher Company: Old cover for MI6 headquarters.

mouchard (French): Double agent.

notional agent: A fictitious agent. At the outbreak of World War II British counterintelligence was able to round up all the German *Abwehr* spies in England. A number were executed. Others were "turned around" to broadcast back chicken feed provided by their captors. There was a risk that these might reveal they were under British control, such as by failing to transmit prearranged errors indicating all was well. So the "turned" agents then "recruited" imaginary ones who provided new chicken feed and, like real agents, demanded ever more money. The notional agents were more reliable than the real ones.

Passport Control Department: For years the MI6 cover in British diplomatic establishments.

la Piscine: The French secret service, so called because its building overlooks an outdoor swimming pool in the Parc des Tourelles.

pocket litter: The usual contents of pockets, carefully assembled to support an agent's cover.

provocation (CIA), **provokatsiya** (KGB): Stirring up a target to see what is revealed or to create embarrassment.

raven (KGB): Male entrapment agent.

rezident: KGB or GRU country spy chief (an embassy has both). Sometimes based in neighboring country. May be under official or nonofficial cover.

SIS: Secret Intelligence Service; Britain's CIA.

Sovbloc green (red): MI6 designation that an agent is not (is) known to the Soviet bloc services.

spy dust: Nitrophenylpentadienal or NPPD. Yellow-white powder said to have been left on doorknobs, etc., by the KGB to track U.S. embassy employees in Moscow.

SS: Security Service; Britain's FBI.

swallow (swallow's nest) (KGB): A female entrapment agent (and her lair, usually fitted with video and sound-recording equipment).

tail-wise: A subject whose behavior shows that he is worried by the possibility of surveillance.

tank (CIA): Secure, insulated conference chamber within a station.

Italian

A Renaissance tale describes a young painter with a beautiful wife, of whom he was exceedingly fond and, alas, jealous. In his canvases this painter usually depicted the Devil as a *signore*: with youthful *disinvoltura*, curly haired, ears scarcely pointed at all, only the hint of a tail. Gratified, the Devil appeared to the painter in a dream. "I'll grant you one wish, *maestro*," he said. "Anything you like." The painter was delighted and explained that he was much vexed by jealousy of his wife's coquettishness. Could His Excellency, magari, help him out in that department?

"*Ma certo, caro, certo,*" said the Devil affably. "Here, take this ring. While it's on your finger you need never fear for the fidelity of your wife. Good luck!" With a barely perceptible whiff of smoke the Devil vanished, and the painter woke from his dream.

He then found that in his sleep his hand, and particularly one finger, had strayed over toward his consort and come to rest in a most intimate location. How could he withdraw it without waking her? And to be sure, what the Devil had said was true, but was it useful?

The Renaissance poet offers his own opinion: so infinite are the wiles of women, that had the painter's wife wished to deceive him, surely she could have done it even then.

attaccabottoni: "Buttonholer": a gloomy bore.

brutta figura: "Ugly face": being made to look bad.

carità pelosa: "Hairy generosity": generosity with an ulterior motive.

cavoli riscaldati: "Reheated cabbage": A defunct love affair, hard to revive.

cicisbeo: Recognized lover of a married woman.

cornuto: "Horned," i.e., "cuckolded": very frequent insult between men.

disinvoltura: An elegantly casual turnout.

furbo: Approving term for ability to outwit others, particularly the authorities. The perfection of *furbizia* is Gianni Schicchi, in Puccini's opera of the same name.

imbroglione: Usually unsuccessful conniver.

in petto: "In his heart": said of a cardinal whose elevation the pope has decided but not announced.

insomma: "To sum up": quite often, and oddly, said after a conversational silence.

iperturistificazione: "Hypertouristification": grossly excessive mass tourism—the problem of Venice.

magari: Odd, constantly used expression, originally ancient Greek. "Is it true you won the lottery?" "*Magari!*" i.e., "If only it were so." But also, if in mid-sentence, "Perhaps."

mbé: Familiar expletive indicating vague doubt.

mò: Expletive of dismay.

partito in quarta: "Off in high gear": i.e., in a rush.

perpetua: A priest's housekeeper . . . or mistress.

ponte: Or (French) *pont*: an extra day off, to connect a Thursday or Tuesday holiday to the weekend.

rompiscatole: "Boxes (balls) breaker": a dreadful bore.

un signore: Untranslatable. Implies easy, elegant cultivated authority, more so than French "*un monsieur.*" Since "gentleman," particularly in America, now means simply "male," and may indeed refer to a habitual felon, the thought has become hard to render. Perhaps "*real* gentleman," but including learning, wit, and a fortunate position.

va fan culo: "Up your ———": used all too frequently, even by children.

Japanese

A pregnant silence, unspoken communication, between men of strong spirit, or *hara*, is called *haragei*. A famous example occurred in 1867. The Tokugawa shogunate, after 264 years and fifteen generations of shoguns, was confronted by the emperor Matsuhito, who demanded that the imperial dynasty recover power. Battle lines were drawn, with the Tokugawas holding the palace area of Tokyo, and the emperor's faction preparing to burn the city to the ground if necessary to dig them out.

The climax of the crisis was a confrontation between Admiral Kaishu Katsu (whose name, fortuitously, means "sea victory"), representing the shogunate, and General Saigo, representing the emperor, who was demanding that the Tokugawas be handed over in person.

Both men knelt across a *tatami* in the formal position, swords lying flat on the left side, and bowed slightly. Tea was served, and according to some accounts, they exchanged a few words. Then they looked steadily at each other, thinking forcefully, projecting *hara*.* After an hour or so of silence, Saigo slapped his thigh. This

*Jalaludin Rumi has a wonderful poem on this theme.
"What if a man cannot be made to say anything:
How do you learn his hidden nature?"
The youngest brother replies:
"I sit in front of him in silence.
I set up a ladder made of patience.
And if in his presence a language from beyond joy
And beyond grief begins to pour from my chest,
I know that his soul is as deep and bright
as the star Canopus rising over Yemen."

Rumi, Mathnawy VI

was taken to signify that he would not insist on the Tokugawas being handed over. The two officers bowed again, silently rose, and departed.

Thereupon the shogunate vacated the palace under safe conduct, and the Meiji era began.

arubeitu: A second job, from German *Arbeit*, "work."

aware: Touched by the ephemeral beauty of the world.

canban: "Just in time": reducing capital requirements by having suppliers deliver parts as needed, rather than maintaining a large inventory.

giri: Honoring one's moral duty: the glue of society.

hachimaki: Headbands worn by members of a group with a tough assignment requiring special concentration and strength, from cram school students and sushi preparers to kamikaze pilots.

hara: Perhaps "stature" or "spirit." Literally, "guts." *Hara-kiri* is "slit guts." A man of large *hara* is ´big-hearted: resolute, sincere, generous, trusting, forgiving, and self-sacrificing . . . the samurai virtues.

honne: One's inner self, as distinct from the outward persona.

ki-ai: The "soul-cry" that accompanies a karate blow.

ma: Significant space, whether in time (a meaningful pause) or between objects (see **Zwischenraum** page 47).

mokusatsu: Kill by pigeonholing.

nemawashi: Creating a consensus, so that the final decision is easy. (Literally, trimming a tree's roots in preparation for transplanting.)

Hachimaki

on: The eternal obligation imposed by certain relationships, e.g., child to parent or student to teacher.

oyabun: The father figure in a group, of large *hara*, who builds loyalty and sets the tone.

A famous old Chinese (not Japanese) example of such leadership concerns a certain General Wu, who was a soldier's soldier and always marched alongside his troops rather than riding. One day he looked into the ranks and saw a man limping. "Fall out!" he ordered. Examining the man's leg, he found an infected cyst.

"Doesn't look good," muttered the general, peering at it. He took his knife, lanced the cyst, and squeezed out most of the contents. Frowning, he put his mouth to the wound and sucked out the rest, spitting it away with a wry face. "Wrap that up and get back in the column," he told the soldier. "Let's see if it gets better."

This story made the rounds of the army, and in time got back to the soldier's home village. The neighbors came to his mother's cabin to felicitate her on this signal attention to her son by the great man. She heard the story, and then, with a disconsolate wail, disappeared indoors, sobbing. The neighbors were puzzled. "What's the matter? Aren't you happy? Your son's famous!"

Through her tears the mother explained: "My husband also marched with this same General Wu, who in fact once performed a similar service for him. From that moment on, my husband would never leave the general, and was killed at his side during a siege. I shall never see my son again!"

In Japanese terms, Wu was an *oyabun*, a boss of large spirit.

sabi: A highly prized quality of discreetly crude, even rusty, simplicity.

seppuku: The more usual word for what Westerners call *hara-kiri*.

shibui: Beauty that reflects time or experience.

tashinamu: Devotion to a cause without regard to the prospect of success or recognition.

wa: Extreme reluctance to be jarring, whence bows, smiles, deferential manners and speech.

wabi: An imperfection that gives an object distinctive elegance. Reflects the Japanese fondness for the apparently rough and unstudied.

yakuza: There are large, well-organized companies (*gumi*) of gangsters (*yakuza*) in Japan, complete with company pins and business cards. The largest single gang, the Yamaguchigumi, is about ten thousand strong.

yoin: An experience imparting deep emotional reverberations. Literally, the sound a bell continues to make long after it is struck.

Language

"I've heard nothing so far from Number Ten," said the ambassador.

Bill Buckley swiveled toward the audience and explained with an amiable leer, "That's where the prime minister lives. It's like saying that you haven't heard from the White House . . . synecdoche."

"It isn't, actually," said the ambassador.

"Oh?" said Buckley, swiveling back in his direction and sardonically raising his eyebrows.

"That would be metonymy," said the ambassador, pleasantly.

The eyebrows stayed aloft, but Buckley's leer evaporated.

alexandrine: A six-foot iambic line.

apocope: "Cutting off" the end of a word: e.g., from automobile to auto, or university to varsity.

aposiopesis: "Falling silent": e.g., "That damned . . ."

apostrophe: "Turning away": addressing someone or something that isn't there.

catachresis: "Misuse" of words: e.g., "presently" for "now," "hopefully" for "let us hope."

dactyl: "Finger": the waltz meter: um—pa—pa.

enjambment: "On-treading": when a phrase runs over the end of a verse couplet into the next one.

hacek: An inverted circumflex accent over *c* or *s* in some languages, e.g., Czech.

hypocorism: Child's prattle: moo-moo, hanky, pinky, toidy.

iamb: "Invective"—because used in satires: metrical foot, e.g., "The *boy* stood *on* the *bur*ning *deck*."

litotes: "Frugality": e.g., "not bad."

metonymy: "Name change": an attribute for the thing itself, e.g., the Vatican for the Pope.

oxymoron: "Sharp-dull": joining two terms of opposite meaning, e.g., sophomore, "wise fool."

schwa: The unaccented vowel sound in English is not pronounced clearly. The last syllable in the words senator and butter should sound alike. In phonetics, this sound is rendered ə, a symbol called the schwa.

synecdoche: The part for the whole. "There'll be ten guns," i.e., hunters: the gun plus the man.

synesis: "Meaning": following the sense instead of strict grammar, e.g., "those sort of thing."

tilde: The Spanish ˜, as in mañana.

Law

"You may cross-examine, Mr. District Attorney," said the judge.

"Mr. Porco, you seem to have your testimony worked out very neatly indeed," said the D.A., rising. "I suppose counsel for the defense told you just what to say and how to say it?"

"Nah, nuttin' like that."

"Well, they rehearsed you a number of times?"

"Nah."

"Once, at least?"

"Nah, nah."

"The defense didn't know ahead of time how you were going to testify?"

"Nah."

"Then why did they call you as a witness? Who asked you to come here today? I remind you that you are under oath. Do you know the penalty for perjury?"

Porco, trapped, was silent.

barratry: A lawyer fomenting unnecessary litigation.

certiorari: Request from a higher court to a lower one to review the transcript of a case.

cestui que trust: The remainderman.

cestui que use: The income beneficiary.

cestui que vie: The "measuring life" of a trust; in England, often the last survivor of the then living descendants of Queen Victoria.

champerty: A lawyer promoting a lawsuit and sharing in its proceeds without being a proper party to it.

cui bono: "Who benefits": a question asked of a crime.

cy pres: Taking the nearest equivalent to a trust condition that can no longer be fulfilled. For instance, a requirement that a scholarship be awarded to "freed slaves" and the funds invested in "streetcar companies" might be altered to read "minorities" and "transportation stocks."

habeas corpus: "You have the body": writ ordering that an accused be produced promptly for trial.

in terrorem: Clause in a will cutting out any beneficiary who contests its provisions.

scire facias: "Make known": writ demanding why a judicial order should not be enforced.

ultra vires: "Beyond his powers": an undertaking beyond one's authority, e.g., I include your property in my will.

venire facias: "Make them come": writ ordering the sheriff to assemble a jury (of veniremen).

Magic

Cruise ship magician: And now, ladies and gentlemen of the audience, one of my finest effects!

Engine room: BOOM! (Ship explodes.)

Furious woman in water, to bedraggled magician, floating nearby: Kee-RIST! Whatsa matter wicha? You some kinda NUT?

black art: A basic principle of illusionary magic: a folding mirror is placed in front of an object to be concealed in a box lined with black velvet. When the door of the box is opened, the viewer sees only shadow—reflected black velvet.

effect: Magician's name for a trick.

force: A pass in which a member of the audience finds it almost impossible not to take the intended card, or to return it except to the intended place in the deck.

head act: Two performers, one on stage and one in the audience, feign telepathic communication.

pass: The key unseen move in a trick.

slick ace or **eel:** A spot of grease on an ace so the deck cuts to it easily.

stripper deck: A slightly tapered deck, which lets the operator extract a card put back in the wrong direction.

Mating

"The appetency of the mare," says Blaine, "is vulgarly called horsing, the bitch goes to heat, the cow to bull, the fox and the hare clicket, the doe ruts, the wolf goes to match or mate, the wild boar and sow, and in some countries the badger also, brims, the rabbit goes to buck, the hare the same, or it clickets. . . ."

Animals **cover, couple,**
  or **pair.**
Birds **tread.**
Boars **brim.**
Fish **spawn.**
Foxes **clickit.**
Hares or coneys **go to buck.**
Harts or bucks **rut** or
  make their vaut.

Hawks **cawk.**
Otters **hunt for their kind**
  or **grow salt.**
Rams **blissom.**
Roes **tourn.**
Turtles **toy** or **tup.**
Wolves **match** or **make.**

Medicine

Harvey Cushing and William Osler were dining at the Somerset Club, following one of Osler's lectures at the College of Physicians and Surgeons.

"The chief difference between man and the animals," declared Sir William exuberantly, "is man's erroneous conviction that he can improve his lot through the use of medicine, and the first duty of the physician is to disabuse him of this pernicious notion. Our one reliable ally is the *vis medicatrix naturae*."

"Osler . . . Osler . . . ! I . . . I never heard . . ."

"Indeed," continued the great English physician imperturbably, "no reasonable man can doubt that witch doctors are not only the best doctors but perhaps the only good doctors. Since medicine—or at least what presents itself as medicine, ninety-nine percent of which is claptrap—undoubtedly does more harm than good on balance, at least psychological therapy, which is the kind practiced by your witch doctors and shamans, has the merit of being noninvasive and thus less dangerous than, for instance, resecting the intestine, or for that matter dosing it."

"But Osler—" cried Cushing.

"I tell you, Cushing," pronounced Osler, "if there is one thing I have learned in half a century of practice, it is the supreme merit of Hippocrates' dictum, 'You shall do no harm.' All these analgesics, antiflatulents, laxatives, aphrodisiacs, cold remedies, diuretics, fertility nostrums . . . humanity would be far, far better off without them. Can you doubt that ancient medicine did more harm than good? Of course not! Rightly is Louis XIV's doctor, Fagon, known as the Killer of Princes. He decimated the Bourbons as thoroughly as the guillotine. Why—"

"But Osler, this is monstrous! You strike at the very heart of our calling!"

"And what of it? Should not a philosopher point out that wars are evil, although there are good generals? Ninety-nine percent of health is common sense, a sensible regimen, a moderate manner of life. Medicine may provide the other one percent, but is as likely to do harm as good, and the harm may be catastrophic, while the good is marginal. So our first task is to point out to our patients where the truth lies in this matter. Our second is to observe, to explain, to reassure, and, eventually, to console. Indeed, my own preferred *modus operandi* is to look wise, say nothing, and grunt."

Pale with anger, Cushing held his peace but resolved to forget his offer to sponsor Osler as a corresponding member of the Massachusetts Medical Society and an honorary member of the Somerset. "Some port, Sir William?" he said, icily.

Osler caught the shift. "With pleasure, Dr. Cushing," he replied.

"We will take it in the library," said Cushing, throwing down his napkin.

acrophobia: Fear of heights.

agoraphobia: Fear of open spaces.

ailurophobia: Fear of cats.

alopecia nervosa: The hair turns white in patches and drops out, usually to regrow in time. Take a trip.

Assher syndrome: J. A. K. Assher studied the Cullinan diamond (3,106 carats—roughly the size of an orange) for nine months in 1908, trying to decide how to cut it. A mistake could have shat-

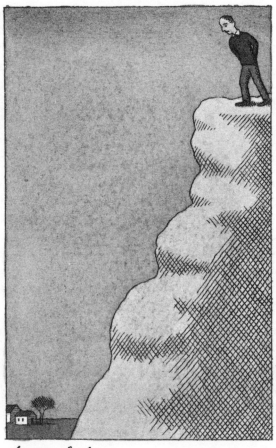

Acrophobia

tered the stone, rendering it worthless. Finally he made up his mind: Whack! With that, he fainted dead away. He thus gave his name to the pattern of extreme concentration followed by unconsciousness. Once cut and polished, the Cullinan joined the British crown jewels.*

Capgrass syndrome: You become utterly convinced that one of your nearest and dearest has been carried off and a ringer substituted.

coprolalia: Talking endlessly about shit.

débridement: Cutting away dead or infected tissue from a wound.

de Clerambault's syndrome: A passionate imaginary love affair, most typically encountered among women in their thirties. Dr. David Enoch, psychiatrist at the Royal Liverpool Hospital, describes a sufferer who invited guests to an elaborate and expensive wedding breakfast—without having enlisted a bridegroom. One unfortunate woman was utterly certain that King George V was sending her signals from Buckingham Palace by adjusting the curtains in particular ways from within.

épluchage: Digging out the foreign matter—e.g., shotgun pellets —from a wound.

Erb's sign: Your heartbeat speeds up when you sit down. (Wilhelm Heinrich Erb, 1840–1921, Heidelberg neurologist.)

*The Great Mogul diamond (280 carats) was lost in New Delhi in 1739, perhaps the most valuable object ever mislaid.

Heimlich's maneuver: Reaching from behind a choking person, you make a fist with one hand and with the other hand violently pull it into his abdomen below the sternum to pop out the obstruction.

koro: Epidemics of this hysterical delusion run through Asia. A man becomes convinced that his penis is retracting into the abdomen, whereupon he will die. With a reliable older woman friend of his wife clutching the vanishing member under a lap-robe, a Malaysian gentleman will ride around town from one doctor to another. A cure is found in time and the victim survives.

In his anxiety he seizes the organ and may fasten it with a pin or tie it with a string. A corresponding condition sometimes occurs in women, when there is a sensation of shriveling of the labia of the vulva and shrinking of the breasts; also known as shook jong.
Stedman's Medical Dictionary

mandarin crease: Runs below each side of the mouth.

Marcus Gunn syndrome: (Also called jaw-winking) The eyelids widen and narrow as you chew.

Müller's maneuver: Valsalva's maneuver in reverse: you suck in, holding your nose.

philtrum: The vertical gutter above the upper lip.

psittacosis: Disease contracted from a parrot bite, or by breathing dust from the bottom of its cage.

rictus: The grin of a corpse.

risorius of Santorini: The muscle that pulls the corners of the mouth up in a smile. Dr. Oliver Wendell Holmes, Sr. (the autocrat, not the jurist), annoyed by some persons' propensity to smile excessively, declared that if he were thus afflicted, he would have it cut out. (Giovanni Domenico Santorini, 1681–1737, Venetian physician and anatomist.)

solar plexus: A term apparently coined by heavyweight champ "Gentleman Jim" Corbett's doctor. A network of nerves supplying the stomach, liver, gall bladder, pancreas, etc.

de la Tourette's syndrome: The victim cannot stop spouting dirty words.

triage: Particularly in battlefield medicine, separating the hopeless cases, usually by giving them a big dose of morphine and laying them quietly to one side, from those who can be treated by the limited facilities available.

Valsalva's maneuver: When you hold your nose and blow out your cheeks in an elevator or airplane to relieve pressure in the ears. (Antonio Maria Valsalva 1666–1723, Bolognese surgeon and anatomist.)

vector: A carrier of germs to humans, e.g., an insect.

vis medicatrix naturae: The spontaneous healing power of nature.

Military

Moosbrugger shifted course right thirty degrees . . . to hit the four enemy destroyers port to port. Gun and torpedo fire-control solutions were cranked in as the unseeing enemy cooperated with steady course and speed. Just seven minutes later the range was four miles. With lookouts estimating the visibility at two miles in the blackness of night, it was time to act. Moosbrugger gave the order to fire, simple and unambiguous, setting all the tactical flywheels of his semiautomatic plan churning in synchronization. The portside torpedoes—twenty-four in all—hit the water from three ships. There was a firing range of sixty-three hundred yards for a running range of four thousand yards—as good a setup as could be expected and all one could ask for. A minute later a "turn nine" order came from Moosbrugger. His division executed a simultaneous ninety-degree turn to starboard to clear out, combing the wakes of the predictable enemy torpedo counterattack. At the same time Simpson wheeled his three destroyers to port and bored in.

The . . . Japanese destroyers scarcely knew what hit them.

Captain Wayne P. Hughes, Jr., *Fleet Tactics: Theory and Practice*

à la guerre comme à la guerre: "In war as in war"—the equivalent of "When in Rome . . ." War has its horrible usages, such as plundering towns that resist, or machine-gunning men who escape from tanks or submarines, which themselves can't take prisoners.

appliqué armor: Supplementary armor attached to vehicles. The ultimate is the reactive armor now on Soviet tanks: essentially boxes of explosives that detonate when hit by an incoming round, to prevent it from penetrating the tank.

boomer: A missile submarine.

the Brigade: The Brigade of Guards: the Grenadier, Coldstream, Scots, Irish, and Welsh Guards (all infantry). The Household Cavalry is the Life Guards and Royal Horse Guards. The two together constitute the Household (or Guards) Division.

C^2, C^3, C^3I: Command and Control; Command, Control and Communications; the latter plus Intelligence.

C.E.P.: Circular error probable: the measurement of a missile's accuracy.

la chamade: The drumbeat or flag by which a fortress signaled its readiness to surrender.

château general: In World War I, a general who ran his division far from the lines. "As we passed the General's white château Dottrell speculated . . . that they must suffer terribly from insomnia with so many guns firing fifteen miles away." (Siegfried Sassoon, *Memoirs of an Infantry Officer*)

combing the wakes: Under torpedo attack one turns parallel to the course of the incoming fish, to offer the smallest possible target.

crossing the T: In pre-missile naval warfare, a cardinal tactical objective was to cross in front of the enemy ship or line. Your entire broadside could bowl down the length of the target, while only their bow armament could reach you.

defeating the enemy in detail: Splitting an enemy force into fragments that can then be destroyed piecemeal.

enfilade: "Getting your ducks in a row": When the beaten zone of artillery or small-arms fire lies along the main axis of the target, or is end on, in ordinary speech. See **crossing the T**. The target is defiladed when it lies perpendicular to the beaten zone.

in the loop: In the sequence of military decision making.

Lanchester equation: Battle casualties between two closely matched formations were once likely to be proportionate to the forces, since combat was essentially a man-to-man or ship-to-ship affair. In other words, if a force of 20,000 men engaged one of 10,000, each might lose 1,000 men. With modern firepower, the larger force of 20,000 may wipe out the smaller one altogether while losing, say, only 4,000 men. This is described in Lanchester's equation. As the smaller force is progressively destroyed, the larger one immediately turns its weapons on the diminishing survivors until they are gone.

LOC (line of communications): An army burns up enormous quantities of munitions, which are hauled forward continually from its base by an umbilical cord of transport vehicles. As the force advances farther from its base this line of communications becomes increasingly vulnerable to attack by the defenders, who enjoy "interior lines." Thus, MacArthur's landing at Inchon forced the evacuation of the lower part of the Korean peninsula by cutting the North Koreans' LOC.

low-intensity conflict: Subversion, insurrection, across-the-border raids, and the like.

platform: Air Force or Navy term for plane or vessel.

salvo chasing: After a warship fires a salvo, the spotters report to fire control whether it fell to the right or left of the target, and whether short or over, and the aim is adjusted. At the receiving end, the captain of the target vessel may well dash toward the last salvo to defeat the adjustment.

tube: Artillerist's term for gun (not rifle) barrel.

Multitudes

The jargon of every occupation includes specialized terms of multitude, such as a *fleet* of ships, a *portfolio* of securities, and a *congregation* of worshippers. Country folk and hunters have group terms for almost every bird and beast. Most of the following are of ancient origin; many are still in current use.

A **colony** of ants
A **shrewdness** or **troop** of apes
A **pace** of asses
A **cete** of badgers
A **shoal** of bass
A **sloth** of bears
A **colony** of beaver*
A **grist, hive** or **swarm** of bees
A **dissimulation** or **volary** of birds
A **singular** of boar (from *sanglier*, "boar," thus a reduplication)
An **army** of caterpillars
A **clouder** of cats (also **clowder, clodder, cludder,** and **clutter**)
A **drove** of cattle

A **brood** or **peep** of chickens (but a **clutch** of eggs)
A **clattering** of choughs
A **rag** of colts
A **covert** of coot
A **herd** of crane
A **murder** of crows
A **cowardice** of curs
A **trip** of dotterel
A **dole** (or **dule**) or **piteousness** of doves or turtledoves
A **flight** of doves (flying)
A **paddling** or **leash** of duck (swimming)
A **raft** of duck (collected in a body in the water)
A **team** of duck (flying)
A **herd** of elephants
A **gang** of elk

When animals are thought of as game, the s is often omitted from the plural.

A **business** of ferrets or flies (This is the term in the fifteenth-century *Book of St. Albans*, the *locus classicus* of these terms. It got corrupted little by little over the centuries to "freaming.")

A **charm** of finches

A **draught** (originally shoal) of fish

A **brace** (two) or **leash** (three) of foxes

A **skulk** or **troop** (or **cloud** or **earth**) of foxes (which, however, are usually solitary)

A **gaggle** of geese (on the ground)

A **skein** of geese (flying)

A **trip** (or **tribe**) of goats

A **charm** or **trimming** or **trembling** of goldfinches

A **band** of gorillas

A **cluster** of grasshoppers

A **pack** of grouse

A **colony** of gulls

A **down** of hares

A **husk** of hares

A **herd** of harts

A **cast** (two) of hawks

A **kettle** of hawks (a large flock)

A **brood** of hens

A **siege** (or **sege**) of herons

A **drift** of hogs

A **harras** of stud horses (still used in Latin languages)

A **couple, cry,** or **mate** of hounds

A **pack** of hounds is twenty-six **couple,** or fifty-two hounds

A **swarm** of insects

A **party** or **band** of jays

A **mob** or **troop** of kangaroos

A **drove** of kine

A **kindle** or **litter** of kittens

A **deceit** of lapwings

An **exaltation, ascension,** or **bevy** of larks

A **leap** of leopards

A **pride** of lions

A **plague** or **swarm** of locusts

A **tidings** of magpies

A **flush** or **sord** of mallards

A **stud** (*sic*) of mares

A **richness** of martens

A **nest** of mice

A **labour** of moles

A **troop** or **shrewdness** of monkeys

A **barren** of mules
A **watch** of nightingales
A **parliament** of owls
A **fling** of oxbirds
A **team** or **yoke** of oxen
A **covey** or **litter** of
  partridge
A **muster** or **ostentation**
  of peacocks
A **bouquet** of pheasant
  (flying)
A **nye** or **covey** of pheasant
  (on the ground)
A **congregation** of plovers
A **string** of ponies
A **litter** of pups
A **covey** or **bevy** of quail
A **nest** of rabbit
A **route** of rats
An **unkindness** of ravens
A **crash** of rhinoceroses
A **bevy** of roebucks
A **building** of rooks
A **murmuration** of sand-
  pipers or starlings

A **pod** of seal (or **harem**,
  if females)
A **flock** of sheep
A **dopping** (meaning "div-
  ing") of shelduck
A **bed** of snakes
A **wisp** or **walk** of snipe
A **host** of sparrows
A **dray** of squirrels (nest)
A **herd** of swans
A **sounder** of swine
A **spring** of teal
A **mutation** of thrush
A **knot** of toads
A **rafter** or **dule** of turkeys
A **bale** of turtles
A **nest** of vipers or wasps
A **pod** or **gam** of whales
A **company** of widgeon
A **pack** or **route** of wolves
A **fall** of woodcock
A **descent** of woodpeckers

Music

Lauritz Melchior, singing in *Lohengrin*, is dismayed to see his swan boat glide off and vanish before he can step into it. Turning to the wings he improvises a bit of *recitativo*: "When does the next swan boat depart?"

bel canto: Vague term for smooth, elegant, agile singing.

bravo: Correctly, *bravo* to a man, and to a woman *brava*.

continuo: A string or keyboard accompaniment for other instruments.

D.C.: (*da capo*) "From the top." When you encounter this instruction, you replay the whole piece to that point.

fake book: A book with just the melody line and chords to a great number of pieces, which enables the band to play them acceptably.

fioritura: Ornamentation of a melody, either by the composer or by the performer.

legato: Smoothly: a direction to the performer.

Ohrwurm: "Earworm": A popular tune that people catch like an infection.

recitative, recitativo: A spoken passage in a choral piece.

segue: To glide from one piece into another.

solfeggio or **solfège:** An exercise using the "sol–fa" syllables (*do re mi fa sol la ti*) for the tones of the scale.

V.T.R.: Vamp till ready: The band or pianist vamps—improvises—until the singer comes on. Middle English *vampe* from Old French *avantpie*: "foot forward."

Bluebeard gig

Political Campaigns

Bluebeard gig: The candidate chats up elderly voters.

cross-pollination: A romance with a rival candidate's staff member.

droolers: Campaign workers who won't work.

moo-moo: A roast beef money-raising dinner.

raisins or **critters:** Older voters.

safe sex: A romance with a fellow-worker for one's own candidate.

tree-huggers or **birds and bunnies:** The environmental lobby.

twilight zoners: Voters who cannot decide between candidates.

Publishing

You're grinding out your weekender in your tiny, hot office in Cairo watching the fan stir the strips of telex traffic hanging from spikes on the wall when the instrument starts to chatter: SHAH OF IRAN FLEES COUNTRY SEND THREE THOUSAND WORDS SOONEST GOLDBERG—your regional editor in Paris. "Another stupid thumbsucker! What am I supposed to know about the goddamn Shah of Iran?" you mutter, pulling down some reference books from the shelf, your scheme of a trip to the desert with the luscious Farida rapidly fading.

bing: Exclamation point.

bladder: The shape containing the words coming from the mouths of cartoon characters.

bulldog: A paper's late-night edition.

bullet: A dot at the start of a paragraph.

cast off: Count the pages of a manuscript to estimate the length of a book.

cruise the queues: (Journalism) examine unpublished stories in the computer.

dial it back: (Journalism) simplify.

doping (a newspaper): Deciding which story will run in what position.

ears: The boxes on either side of the name of a newspaper, e.g., the one containing the legend "All the news that's fit to print."

grabber: The opening words of a column or article, in which the writer tries to capture the reader's interest.

gutter: The vertical division between the left and right pages.

nut: Transitional paragraph (usually about the fourth) where the lead passes into the body of the story.

over the transom: Unsolicited manuscript.

phat: Probably from "fat": profitable; a layout with a lot of white space.

quote boy: The person who digs out hundreds of appropriate quotations to stuff like plums in a pudding into books by businessmen and politicians.

river: White space down the middle of a printed page, formed by the pattern of spaces between words.

sidebar: A box within an article.

silver fork fiction: About rich, prominent people.

slot: The center of the City Room.

thumbsucker: A "think piece"—long on vague conjecture and short on hard news.

TK: From "to come"—more material to follow.

violin: The lead story, which sets the tone of an issue of a magazine.

weekender: Feature intended as stuffing for Sunday edition.

widow: A word or partial word overflowing a paragraph (e.g., "azine" following **violin** above).

zipper: Newspaper article running down entire middle column.

Racing

boat race: Two harness racers box in the favorite to let another horse break through.

break the maiden: Win the first race entered for.

claiming race: In a $10,000 claiming race, any entrant can be bought for $10,000.

daisy cutter: Doesn't lift its feet.

early foot: Starts fast.

flying change: Changing leads while running. If a racehorse doesn't change leads, the pounding may damage the lead foot.

mudder: Runs well on a muddy track.

plater: A cheap horse entered in a **claiming race**.

roarer: Breathes loudly.

side-wheeler: Trotting man's term for a pacer.

Thoroughbred: Descendants of three horses: the Byerly Turk, the Darley Arabian, and the Godolphin Arabian.

Anchor

Sailing

aboveboard: A disguised pirate vessel approaching a victim would sometimes parade some innocuous figures aboveboard, on deck, while the cutthroats crouched out of sight. If the vessel was innocuous, with no cutthroats, then everything was aboveboard.

admiral: From Arabic *amir-al-bakr* (or *bahr*), king of the sea.

ahoy: The traditional seaman's hail; once a Viking battle cry. *Hoi* is still the blind-corner cry of Venetian gondoliers. When the telephone was first introduced, you started with "ahoy" instead of "hello."

anchor: From Greek *ankura*, in turn from proto-Indo-European.

Beaufort scale: Table of wind velocities, standard among mariners, published in 1805 by Admiral Sir Francis Beaufort.

Beaufort Number	Name	Miles per Hour	Description
0	calm	less than 1	calm; smoke rises vertically
1	light air	1–3	direction of wind shown by smoke but not by wind vanes
2	light breeze	4–7	wind felt on face; leaves rustle; ordinary vane moved by wind
3	gentle breeze	8–12	leaves and small twigs in constant motion; wind extends light flag

Beaufort Number	Name	Miles per Hour	Description
4	moderate breeze	13–18	raises dust and loose paper; small branches are moved
5	fresh breeze	19–24	small trees in leaf begin to sway; crested wavelets form on inland waters
6	strong breeze	25–31	large branches in motion; telegraph wires whistle; umbrellas used with difficulty
7	moderate gale (or near gale)	32–38	whole trees in motion; inconvenience in walking against wind
8	fresh gale (or gale)	39–46	breaks twigs off trees; generally impedes progress
9	strong gale	47–54	slight structural damage occurs; chimney pots and slates removed
10	whole gale (or storm)	55–63	trees uprooted; considerable structural damage occurs
11	storm (or violent storm)	64–72	very rarely experienced; accompanied by widespread damage
12	hurricane	73–136	devastation occurs

Blue Peter: Mariner's name for the International Signal Code letter "P," a blue flag with a white rectangle in its center, indicating that the ship is sailing that day. Peter is probably a corruption of "repeater," the flag used to request that a flag signal from another ship be repeated.

brigantine: In the sixteenth century, any vessel or rig used by the brigands of the French coast and of the West Indies. Came to mean a two-masted vessel with a square-rigged foremast.

charter party: The document setting forth a charter agreement, in two copies, one for the owner and one for the charterer. From French *charte partie*, divided document.

gurry: Originally, fish guts; now any messy accumulation.

head: The latrines were once just forward of the forecastle beakhead, which shrank to "head."

hull speed: A keel sailboat's theoretical maximum speed: about 1.4 times the square root of the wetted waterline. The boat can go faster as it heels over because the wetted waterline is lengthened.

jack: A small flag flown at the bow of a motor vessel at anchor. (The U.S. jack is called, confusingly, the union jack, because it is the "union"—the fifty stars in a blue field—of the national flag.)

lines: Almost never **ropes**, q.v.

listless: In very calm weather, the vessel stays level—doesn't list.

mizzen: From Arabic *miẓein*, balance. The aftermost mast on a two- or three-masted vessel.

Mother Carey's Chickens: Mariner's name for stormy petrels. Perhaps a corruption of Latin *mater cara*, "dear mother," the

Virgin Mary, protector of sailors. Petrel, in turn, may come from (Saint) Peter.

pea jacket: Short jacket of heavy wool. From Dutch *pij*, pronounced pea, a heavy water-repellent wool.

pipe down: Boatswain's (piped) signal to turn in for the night.

rope: A sailor calls working ropes lines. There are only a few "ropes" on a vessel, including the bell rope, man ropes, and bolt ropes.

round robin: From ribbon. Seventeenth-century captains could inflict savage punishment on the instigator of a grievance petition, often the first on the list. These were sometimes signed on a ribbon with its ends joined together, so that there was no "first."

scuttlebutt: Gossip then as now centered on the drinking fountain, formerly a water barrel, or butt, with a small hatch, or scuttle, in it.

sheer: The deck's profile.

skipper: The master. In yachting, "captain" implies a professional.

son of a gun: As late as the eighteenth century, women lived aboard warships. At sea they sometimes slept between the guns. "Begat in the galley and born under a gun," went the saying.

Science

ampulli of Lorenzini: Pits around a shark's snout that detect electrical charges. A shark could theoretically sense a wounded fish a thousand miles away; in fact, of course, sea static prevents this.

angle of repose: Angle beyond which an object will start sliding down an inclined plane.

big bang (crunch): The sudden beginning (end) of the universe.

butterfly effect: It is impossible to foresee the long-range consequences of particular events: "for want of a nail," and so forth. Scientists hypothesize a butterfly over Mount Fuji whose wings create a disturbance in the air that eventually, combined with other influences, turns out to be the ultimate origin of a storm in the Caribbean.

cohort: In demography, a generation.

Coriolis effect: The tendency of objects in a fluid to drift in response to the rotation of the earth, named for Gaspard de Coriolis, French physicist, 1792–1843.

deadly embrace: Two inputters accessing the same computer simultaneously get stuck. Neither can proceed.

the gambler's ruin: Economic theory. A gambler who plays a progression system—increasing his stake every time he loses until finally he wins, when he starts again—must ultimately be wiped out. He will eventually suffer such a disastrous losing streak that he can't get going again.

idols of the:
  tribe (*idola tribus*)
  cave (*specus*)
  marketplace (*fori*)
  theater (*theatri*)

Bacon's classification of fallacies. Our thought and communication are limited by our humanity, by our own nature, by the way words are used at the time, and by the philosophical framework we are working in. The "tribe" is the human mind, the "cave" is personal idiosyncrasy, the "marketplace" is vulgar speech, and the "theater" is systems of philosophy.

kingdom: The classifications are: **kingdom, phylum** (for plants, **division**), **class, order, family, tribe** (not always used for animals), **species,** and **subspecies** (not always used for animals).

laurence: The miragelike shimmering above a paved road under hot sun: presumably from the eponymous saint who was martyred by frying.

monorchidaceous: Possessing only one testicle.

a Munro: Scottish peak over 3,000 feet. Sir Hugh Munro (1856–1919) set forth to climb all 277 of them, but died after only 275.

neutrino: Tiny particles without charge or (probably) mass. You, reader, while perusing this section have been penetrated by a billion or so neutrinos from a supernova—exploding star—of the constellation Andromeda in the Greater Magellanic Cloud called Sanduleap –69°202, or SN 1987-A.

oblate (prolate): The earth is not a perfect sphere but a spheroid; specifically, an oblate spheroid: flattened at the poles. A football is a prolate spheroid: with attenuated poles.

Occam's Razor: William of Ockham (c. 1300–1349) proposed cutting from the analysis of a subject everything extraneous to its essence.

orrery: A mechanical model of the solar system, named after Charles Boyle, fourth Earl of Orrery (1676–1731).

Paradox of Epimenides (a seventh-century Cretan): "All Cretans are liars."

Perseids: A meteor shower, the debris of an exploded comet, seen every mid-August, sometimes as densely as one a minute. In Italian, *la notte di San Lorenzo.*

pH factor: "Potential of hydrogen": the proportion of hydrogen in a solution, expressed on the logarithmic scale.

pons asinorum: "Bridge of asses." A Euclidean proposition that dullards supposedly cannot grasp. By extension, any idea that the mass has trouble understanding.

regress to the mean: The tendency of the unusual to fade back to the usual. The descendants of giants eventually shrink to normal height.

Russell's paradox: Some classes contain themselves, such as "topics of discussion" or "things I forget." Most do not: the *class* of bluebirds is not itself a bluebird. So: Does the class of all classes that do not contain themselves contain itself, or not?

scintillation: The winking of stars—whence, "not a scintilla of evidence."

singularity: In relativity theory, a situation, such as the **big bang,** the **big crunch,** or a black hole, when the density of the universe and space-time curvature become infinite, so that the laws of science, including relativity theory, no longer apply.

strange loop: (Mathematical logic) Self-referential proposition, including the **Paradox of Epimenides**, q.v. For instance, "All generalizations are false, including this one."

time dilation: The relativity concept that time slows as a body approaches the speed of light.

Train's Law: "Price controls increase prices."

widdershins (also **withershins**), **deasil:** Counterclockwise, clockwise.

Shit

Badger, boar, or wolf: **lesses, fiants**
Coney or hare: **buttons, croteys**
Deer: **fumets**
Fox: **billitings, fiants**
Hawk: **mutes**
Hound: **puer**
Man: **shit, ordure, night soil, crap***
Marten: **dirt, fiants**
Otter: **spraints, wedging**

*From Thomas Crapper, inventor of the flush toilet.

Shooting

"Done much shootin'?" General Tolliver asked his guest, a young Austrian whom his daughter had invited for the weekend. Palffy shot regularly at his uncle's and modestly replied, "A bit."

The general explained the routine. The party would set forth on horseback with a pair of pointers a few hundred yards ahead quartering around where they could scent any birds before the noise of the horses put them up. The hounds were a speckled white, for ready visibility. When the covey rose, the gun on the left took the birds on the left, and the gun on the right correspondingly. A skillful gun could often bring off a double.

They mounted and set forth. After a while Bugle and Deuce lowered their noses toward the ground and started moving forward slowly and tensely: "trailing." "They're making game," said the general. Then the first hound pointed, and the second instantly halted and pointed too. "He's backing Deuce," said the general, dismounting.

Palffy slid from his saddle but had trouble pulling his gun from its scabbard. "Come along, suh," muttered the general. "The birds won't hold." Palffy advanced, his gun, now loaded, at the ready. He peered at the ground where the dogs were pointing, while the general gazed blandly into the middle distance. Suddenly, with a wild *whirr*, the covey burst from some cane grass almost behind them. Taken aback, Palffy whirled around. Shooting driven birds in Europe, one aims almost directly overhead; to lower the muzzle toward the ground threatens one's neighbors or the beaters. So Palffy, inhibited from dropping his gun toward the birds, fired wildly and missed. The general, taking his time, picked off a pair that were corkscrewing away from them.

As they returned to the horses, the general looked at his daughter and rolled his eyes slightly upward.

BIRDSHOOTING

backing: When a dog points another dog who is pointing birds. Also called respecting the point.

becking: Calling grouse, or the sound made by cocks when challenging other cocks or humans.

cast-off: The butt of a right-handed shooter's gun bends slightly to the right; this is known as the "cast-off."

choke: A shotgun's left barrel is usually narrower than the right one. Since it is fired second, the bird will have flown farther, requiring a tighter pattern.

improved cylinder: A mild choke.

making game: When the dogs show that they're on to something, usually by moving very cautiously.

towering: When a bird hit in the head flies straight up before falling.

the Twelfth, or **Glorious Twelfth:** August 12, the opening of the grouse season in Scotland.

DEERSTALKING

cromie: Stag with one horn that bends backward.

heavier: Horned stag that cannot reproduce. Said to be a better sentinel than even the most suspicious hind.

hummel: Stag without horns but able to reproduce. Dangerous, because able to butt violently.

McNab: When, in one day, you kill a stag, a brace of grouse and a salmon.*

*A male salmon or other game fish is a **cock**, incidentally.

Cock

squire: Young stag that attaches himself to an older one.

switch: Stag with single long horns. Dangerous because he can easily spike other stags. "Och, he's just a dirty switch," said the gillie to my wife on one occasion.

BIG GAME (India)

dangerous game: Thick-skinned (buffalo, elephant, or rhino); thin-skinned (bear, panther, or tiger).

machan: Elevated platform to shoot from.

nullah: Dried-up stream bed.

shikar (shikari): Game (guide).

spoor: Traces left by game animals.

Sociology

Ah! In the window was a single alarm clock. I entered the little store to find an elderly rabbi behind a bare desk. "My traveling alarm is bust. I need a new one. Do you have a good, loud one, as small as possible?" The rabbi smiled faintly. "I'm a *mohel*," he said. "What's that?" "A *mohel* performs circumcisions according to Jewish ritual." "Oh!" I said. "Sorry. But why do you have an alarm clock in the window?" "What do you want I should put in the window?" answered the *mohel*.

agniology: The philosophical study of ignorance.

arbiter elegantiarum: "Determiner of elegancies": A Beau Brummell or Ward McAllister, who sets the tone of society. Originally referred to Petronius, called Petronius Arbiter.

argumentum ad . . .

    baculum (stick): A threat for an argument.

    crumenam (purse): Appealing to his financial interest.

    hominem: Directed to the listener's personal prejudices.

    ignorantiam: Depending on the hearer's not knowing something essential.

    populum: Pandering to popular passion.

    verecundiam (modesty): One whose response forces the opponent into indecency.

avoska (Russian): "Perhaps"; expandable bags carried by pedestrians for fortuitous purchases.

beard: A lesbian's male **walker**, q.v.

boondoggle: Literally, the leather knot under a Boy Scout's hat.

circumcision style: A calendar beginning January 1, the date of Jesus's circumcision.

cognitive dissonance: The uneasy feeling caused by differences between what is expected and what one perceives.

dead man's hand (poker): Black aces and eights—which Wild Bill Hickok was holding when shot from the back by Crooked Nose Jack McColl in Saloon Number Ten, Deadwood, Dakota Territory. Wild Bill killed about 75 men enforcing his own brand of order.

deuterogamy: A second marriage.

dottle: The lump of tobacco ash left in a pipe bowl.

entryism (Leninist jargon): A Soviet front group's "long march through the institutions" of a target state.

esquire: A gentleman, *not* a lawyer as such. In England, substantial landed proprietor, eldest son of a knight, eldest son of a younger son of a peer, bearer of a coat of arms, holder of a royal warrant, etc. The English have so far been spared the ghastly vulgarity of a female lawyer signing herself "Esq."

feng shui (Chinese): "Wind and water": a system for situating things and buildings in harmony with nature, to give good luck.

fulminate a bull: The pope does not issue a statement, but for important matters, a bull (from *bolla*, seal), which he is said to fulminate.

Beard

geek: A sideshow performer who bites the heads off chickens.

glavni vrag (Soviet): The "main enemy": the United States.

Glorious Revolution: 1688–89, when the English ousted James II and brought in William and Mary.

glottophonoly: Telling the ages of languages by their divergences from a common source.

heir apparent: The eldest (surviving) son. When the holder of a dignity has no son, the next in succession—often a nephew—is called the heir presumptive; he is displaced if a son is then born.

Hobson's choice: No choice. From Thomas Hobson of Cambridge, a seventeenth-century liveryman who would only release his horses in strict rotation.

Homer, birthplace of: Position claimed by (in hexameter) Smyrna, Rhodos, Colophon, Salamis, Chios, Argos, Athenae.

hyperogamy: Marrying above one's station.

kissing gate: A double gate between cow fields. The one behind closes upon you and your companion before the next will open.

lagniappe: In Louisiana, a bonus. From American-Spanish *la ñapa*, from Quechua Indian *yapa*, "addition."

laughing boy: New York expression for a prominent man's hanger-on.

malapropism: From Mrs. Malaprop, in Sheridan's *The Rivals*. One of her contributions to zoology was the news that "allegories live on the banks of the Nile."

man on the box: A footman who rode next to the coachman and opened the doors of the coach and handed down the ladies.

mauve decade: Decadent period, especially the 1890s.

maya (Sanskrit): Confusing a symbol with the reality it represents.

merkin: A pubic wig.

mohel: Jewish ritual circumciser.

morganatic marriage: Nondynastic marriage of a royal or princely person with someone of lower rank.

mulligan: If the drive from the first tee is wild, some golfers give each other a free second try.

Muses: The Nine, daughters of Zeus and Mnemosyne, are Calliope (epic poetry), Clio (history), Erato (lyric poetry and mime), Euterpe (lyric poetry and music), Melpomene (tragedy), Polyhymnia (sacred poetry, singing, rhetoric, and mime), Terpsichore (dancing and choral singing), Thalia (comedy and pastoral poetry), and Urania (astronomy).

orenda (Huron): The power of focused will; the opposite of submission to fate.

parea: A wonderful Greek word, and an interesting custom. An Athenian couple will usually circulate only within their own set— a dozen or so other families, some of them cousins, most of them family friends. A wife joins her husband's *parea* and ordinarily no longer frequents the crowd she knew as a girl. Accepting an invitation for dinner, a Greek woman will ask who's coming. "Oh, the *parea,*" her hostess will reply.

parvel: A priest's mistress.
> *Housekeeper to visitor:* I'm sorry, the bishop is having his nap.
> *Visitor:* I would not presume to disturb his grace in the arms of Morpheus.

Housekeeper: Actually, I think it's Sophie.

Priests have since the Middle Ages been vowed to celibacy—bachelorhood—in part to forestall the temptation to accumulate wealth for their children. Chastity, however, is another matter.

plus fours: Loose knickerbockers overlapping the knees for added freedom in active sports, particularly golf. Derives from the four extra inches of cloth needed below the knee in tailoring.

powder room: Doesn't refer to gunpowder: in the old days one had to repowder one's hair from time to time, a messy procedure.

pushlost: Moral and intellectual obesity, e.g., bad art masquerading as serious art, sentimental twaddle posing as a substantial statement, morally equating aggression with resisting aggression.

rice Christian: Chinese who converts to be fed.

salt and pepper (*oeil de perdrix*): A cloth pattern for men's suitings.

Sebastianism: The belief that a great historical figure will arise and deliver his people. The Portuguese waited for King Sebastian to return after he was killed, and the Rastafarians think Haile Selassie will return in a destroyer to take them home from Jamaica to Ethiopia.

shadow price: The incremental rate of return that would be derived by relaxing a constraint, e.g., enlarging a plant.

shih (Chinese): Knowledge coupled with insight and judgment.

Stockholm syndrome: Emotional dependence on their captors developed by hostages or kidnap victims.

ta (Chinese): To understand things and take them lightly.

taboo deformation: A word so embarrassing to say or ill-omened that people deliberately pronounce it wrongly, e.g., the distortions in English of the German surnames Fuchs (fox) or Koch (cook).

talkin (Indonesian): Whisper instructions to the dying.

tartle: Momentarily fail to recognize someone.

tjotjog (Javanese): "Tjotjog *means to fit, as a key does in a lock, as in medicine a specific remedy does to a disease, as a man does with the woman he marries. . . . If your opinion agrees with mine, we tjotjog. Tasty food, correct theories, good manners, comfortable surroundings, gratifying outcomes are all* tjotjog."

Clifford Geertz, *The Interpretation of Cultures*

the tragedy of the commons: The process by which a grazing area, fishing ground, or forest is overexploited, so that production declines and the users derive less and less benefit from more and more work.

Train's law of exaggeration: "Nothing exceeds like success."

being undone:
   A castle is **slighted**.
   A congressman is **unseated**.
   A currency is **debased**.
   A ghost is **laid**.
   A king is **dethroned**.
   A lawyer is **disbarred**.
   A lover is **discarded**.
   A maiden is **deflowered**.
   An officer is **cashiered**.
   A pope is **deposed**.

A president is **impeached**.
A priest is **un-** or **de-frocked,** or silenced.
A prince is **mediatized**.
A Quaker undergoes **disfellowship**.
A regiment is **disbanded**.
A samurai becomes a **ronin**.
A solicitor is **struck off the rolls**.
An English university student is **rusticated**.
A work of art is **deaccessioned**.

vranyo (Russian): I know perfectly well that he's lying; he knows that I must know; I know that he knows. Still for the moment, we leave it all unsaid.

walker: An older woman's escort to plays, openings, etc.

wet pogrom: An outrage against a minority in which blood is shed. A **dry pogrom** destroys only property.

woop-woop (Australian): The most out-of-the-way possible backwoods settlement.

yeoman: A noted English legal decision held that society consisted of the king, the royal family, dukes, earls, viscounts, barons, baronets, knights, esquires, gentlemen, yeomen, artisans, and peasants. A certain manufacturer, therefore, who had ceased to be an artisan but had not become a gentleman (then defined as a man with no fixed occupation) had perforce to be a yeoman, subject to the rights and obligations of that category.

Tennis

Formerly, and still in some usages, referred to as court tennis (or real tennis). This ancient game, an adaptation of the original tennis beloved of the kings of France and England, is played off all four sides and the floor of a large stone court with a variety of traps and obstacles. Players call the game simply tennis; the familiar game of tennis is properly called lawn tennis, even when played on clay. The "tennis" in the Tennis Court Oath or the Racquet and Tennis Club in New York refers to court tennis, not lawn tennis.

I was playing lawn tennis with him on a damp grass court on the borders of Lyme Regis. I happened to be seeing the ball and for once in my life really was driving it in to that precious square foot in the back-hand corner of the base line. After one of these shots, Simpson was "carried away" enough to tap his racket twice on the ground and cry "chase better than half a yard." I only dimly realized that this was an expression from tennis itself*, which had slipped out by accident; that he was familiar with the great original archetype of lawn tennis, compared with which lawn tennis (he wished to make and succeeded in making me understand) was a kind of French cricket. . . .

Stephen Potter, *Gamesmanship*

ad box, deuce box: The area into which you must put the serve on the ad or deuce side.

ad court, deuce court: The left-hand or right-hand court in lawn tennis.

*I.e., court tennis.

better than (e.g., two): In court tennis, a shot that bounces for the second time closer to the wall than (e.g.) two yards, but not closer than one and a half.

chase: In court tennis, a point held in suspense and replayed after a shot is missed outright.

dedans: The little netted window with a bell in it at the receiver's left in court tennis.

four-baller: A game when all four first serves are in, and the server wins each point.

gallery: The netted enclosures behind the server and under the penthouse in court tennis.

not up: When the ball bounces twice before being returned.

penthouse: In court tennis, the inclined horizontal structure at the server's left: the serve must bounce off it.

railroad: A right-to-left spin service in court tennis.

tambour: The vertical structure at the receiver's left in court tennis.

whirlybird: In both kinds of tennis, a serve hit close to shoulder height with either right-to-left spin or topspin.

wormburner: A hard shot that does not rise from the court.

worse than (e.g., two): In court tennis, a shot that bounces for the second time farther from the wall than (e.g.) two yards, but not farther than two and a half.

Theater

apron: The part of the stage in front of the curtain.

claque: Hired clappers.

come down in one: Step to the front of the stage.

ice: Illegal profits from ticket selling.

off book: In rehearsal, doing without the script. "We went off book today."

scrim: A gauzy drop, opaque if lit from the front and transparent if from behind.

teaser: Side panel advertising the show.

tormenter: Panel across the top of the theater entrance, showing the title of the play and the star.

Wall Street

Belgian dentists: Swiss banking jargon for uninformed exploitable customers.

customer's man: Old term for broker who talks to customer; later, "registered representative" ("registered rep"); still later, "account executive" or, in less scrupulous firms, "consultant."

dead-cat bounce: When the market, which is supposed to rebound 30 percent or so after a crash, instead barely twitches.

efficient market theory: Academically propounded but silly belief that the market reflects all that can be known about a security, so that research is unnecessary.

flower bonds: Treasury bonds that may be presented at par for payment of estate taxes.

greenmail: When a raider is bought out by a company, usually to protect the directors' private prerogatives, at a price not offered to the shareholders generally. A loathsome practice, rendered even more repellent when the raider masks his greed by protestations of high concern for the victims.

green shoe: Overallotment option granted to managing underwriter to purchase an additional 10 to 15 percent of an underwriting.

haircut: Discount, particularly applied to a broker's inventory in computing his net worth.

lollypop: Deterring an unwelcome acquirer by offering to buy out all other shareholders at a premium over market.

mezzanine bracket: The second tier of a tombstone.

mezzanine level: Stage of a company's development just before initial public issue.

Pac-Man: An antitakeover maneuver in which the target firm bites back at the raider by buying up his shares in a counterbid.

painting the tape: Fictitious transactions to create interest in a security.

poison pill: The issuance of preferred stock giving holders the right to redeem it at an enormous premium after a takeover.

porcupine provisions: Corporate bylaws designed to deter takeovers.

rainmaker: Business-getter.

Saturday night special: Takeover maneuver in which raiders suddenly elect their own candidates to the board of directors to take control of a company.

shark repellent: Defensive measure taken by a company to fend off takeovers.

sweat equity: Stock granted for work, rather than paid for in cash.

tailgating: When a securities salesman imitates a customer's transaction.

tombstone: Austere published announcement of securities issue or deal.

watered stock: Shares issued to insiders without sufficient consideration. Refers to cattle-sellers' practice of encouraging beasts to drink before weighing.

yellow peril: Yellow-covered statutory report submitted by insurance company to state insurance commission.

Wine

"First, then, which district in Bordeaux does this wine come from? That is not too difficult to guess. It is far too light in the body to be from either St. Emilion or Graves. It is obviously a Médoc. There's no doubt about that.

"Now—from which commune in Médoc does it come? That also, by elimination, should not be too difficult to decide. Margaux? No. It cannot be Margaux. It has not the violent bouquet of a Margaux. Pauillac? It cannot be Pauillac, either. The wine of Pauillac has a character that is almost imperious in its taste. And also, to me, a Pauillac contains just a little pith, a curious, dusty, pithy flavor that the grape acquires from the soil of the district. No, no. This is a very gentle wine, demure and bashful in the first taste, emerging shyly but quite graciously in the second. A little arch, perhaps in the second taste, and a little naughty also, teasing the tongue with a trace, just a trace, of tannin. Then, in the aftertaste, delightful—consoling and feminine, with a certain blithely generous quality that one associates only with the wines of the commune of Saint Julien. Unmistakably this is a Saint Julien."

Roald Dahl, "Taste"

Like so many promising '85s, the chardonnay is only just emerging from its restrained adolescence, as baked apple, pear, and spice begin to challenge the wood and vanillin of French cooperage. Blossoming varietal fruit also contributes flesh to a fine acid backbone and watch for a hint of youthful spritz in the glass.

Wine list at the Spanish Inn, Pebble Beach, California

Nebuchadnezzar

balance: A harmonious combination of fruit, acidity, and tannin.

barnyard: A disagreeable odor, usually because of dirty barrels or equipment.

blackcurrant: A smell associated with red Bordeaux.

Bottle Sizes:	*Number of bottles*
magnum	2
Jeroboam	4
Rehoboam	6
Methuselah (or **Imperial**)	8
Salmanazar	12
Balthazar	16
Nebuchadnezzar	20

chambrer: Letting wine brought from the cellar warm to room temperature.

charpenté: Smooth, fat.

chewy, fleshy, meaty: With a lot of body; densely textured (often comes from high glycerine content).

closed: Used of a young wine whose full character will not be apparent for several years.

complex: A wine with a variety of tastes and scents . . . ordinarily a merit.

corked: A wine that smells of its own cork, which is presumably dirty or damaged.

corsé: Hard, tannic.

fat: An intense, rich quality, often the result of a sunny, hot summer and autumn.

flinty: Said of Chablis, as is "a whiff of gunpowder."

hard: Rough or acidic. Hardness is not the same as harshness, which is never good, while a hard young wine may be excellent after time.

hazelnuts and butter: The flavor of Meursault.

hot: A high alcohol content that burns the throat.

jammy: With a concentrated, fruity taste.

nose: The smell; what the nonwine person calls the bouquet.

oaky: A toasty, vanilla smell and taste imparted to wine by its aging in oak barrels.

ullage: The evaporation of wine in the bottle. For a 1961 one might expect the wine to be low in the neck, for a 1945 between there and the top of the shoulder, and for a 1927 at midshoulder. Top-quality wines are sometimes uncorked, topped up with the same wine of the same year, and then recorked, so the ullage may not be apparent from the level in the bottle. A chateau will ordinarily recork its own stock every twenty years.

volatile: A wine that smells of vinegar.

wet wool: The sauvignon blanc taste (Sancerre).

Wrong Words

The opposite of the *mot juste* is the wrong word, particularly the pretentious, and thus vulgar, wrong word. On a flight to Phoenix I was mystified when the stewardess, serving roast beef, asked me, "Do you want some onjoo with that?" When I discovered that she had been taught at the American Airlines school to use this way of asking if one wanted the beef *au jus*—with gravy—I wrote the company; eventually this horror was expunged from the curriculum. Good talk and writing is plain, strong, and direct, not pretentious or trendy. For instance, one avoids "gentleman" for "man," or "He told Mrs. Jones and myself" for "He told my wife and me." To a countryman a "bitch* whelps," not a "lady dog has babies." The English call this distinction "U" (upper class, aristocratic) and non-U.

wrong word	good English
apparel	clothes
author† a book, host a dinner	write a book, give a dinner
bubbly	champagne
beautiful human being, lovely person	good man (woman)
beverage (*Waitress*: "Do you want your beverage with the main?")	(something to) drink

*I will not dwell on today's mild paranoia that finds shameful sex in familiar words, the way some Victorians changed "leg" to "limb" and (chicken) "breast" to "white meat." Anyway, a female fisherman is a fisherman, not a fisherperson.
†Using nouns as verbs reveals a desire to impress by trendiness.

131

concerned (e.g., father)	being a good . . .
country house (in England, implies immense pile)	house in the country
drapes	curtains
fabric	material, stuff
freshen up	wash
gentleman (in any sense except a man of superior standing)	man
gown	dress
have a good one, have a nice day	good-bye
I don't recollect, recall	I don't remember
I'm all set	no, thanks
I'm partial to	I like
I've made plans	I'm going out to dinner
inexpensive, reasonable	cheap
lady (when referring to cleaning woman, salesgirl, etc.)	woman, girl
live-in; significant other	lover, mistress
pass on	die
perspire	sweat
quality time	good time together
refined (e.g., person)	well brought up
select or exclusive neighborhood	good part of town
senior citizen	old man, woman
serviette (English)	(table) napkin
settee	sofa
timepiece	watch

townhome (Townhouse for a house not in town is worse than non-U, it is an abomination.)	house
tux	dinner jacket, black tie
wealthy‡	rich
well connected	of good family

‡*I like David Rockefeller's comforting expression "men of wealth" but deplore his and other banks' smarmy term "high net worth individuals."*